Lord's
The Guide

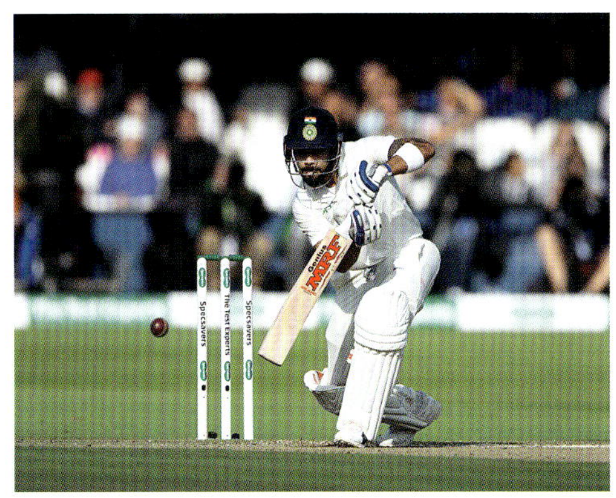

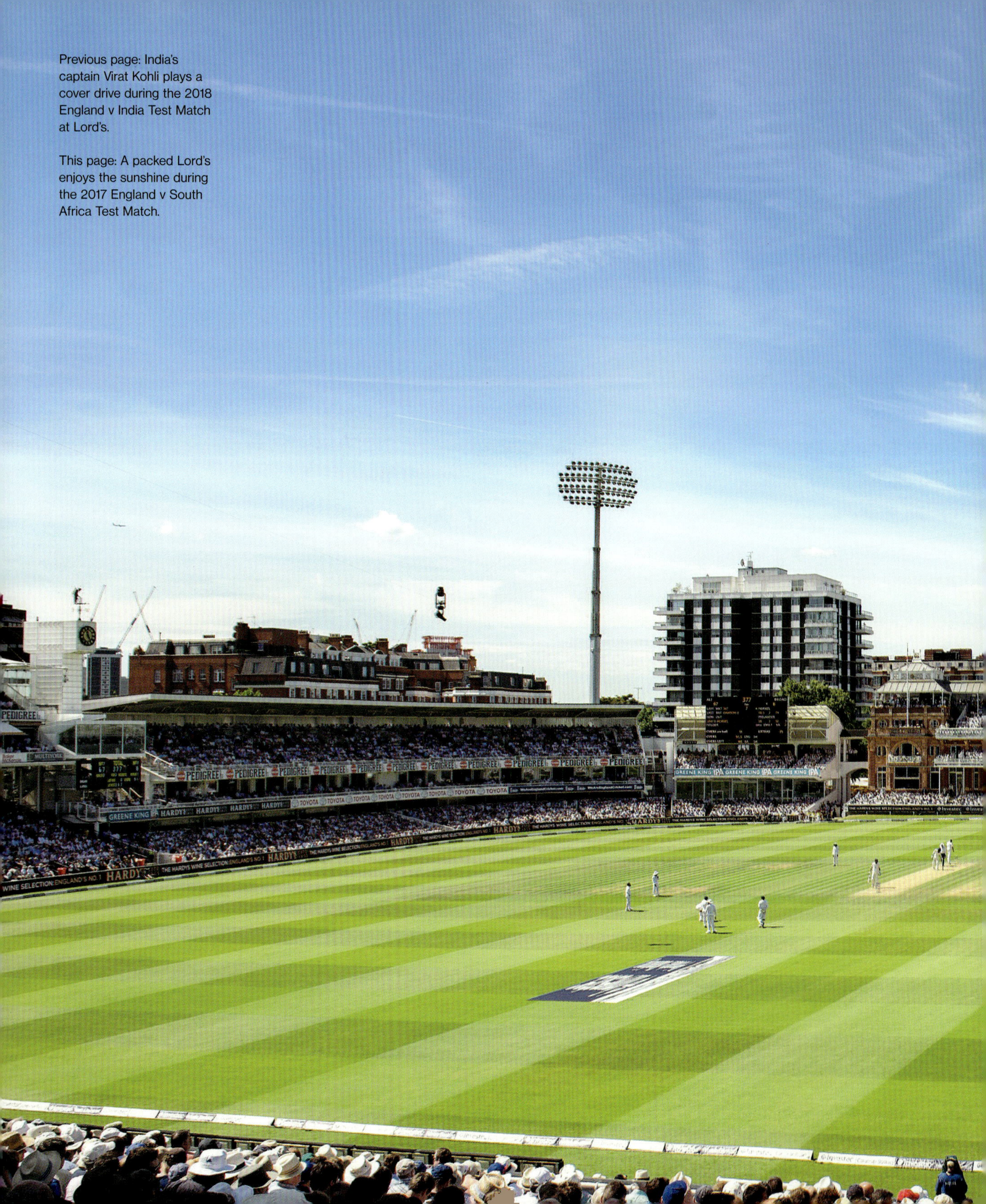

Previous page: India's captain Virat Kohli plays a cover drive during the 2018 England v India Test Match at Lord's.

This page: A packed Lord's enjoys the sunshine during the 2017 England v South Africa Test Match.

Contents

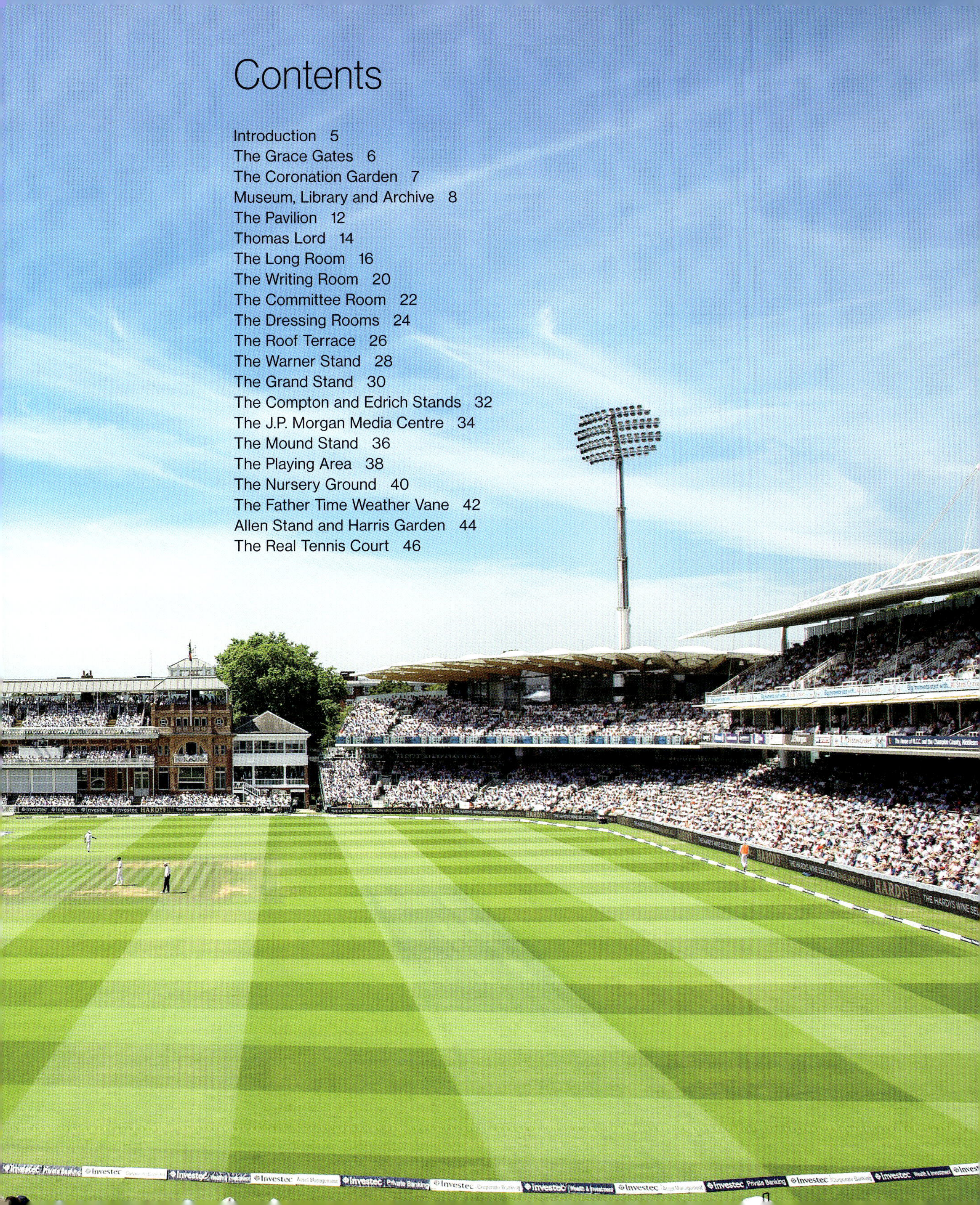

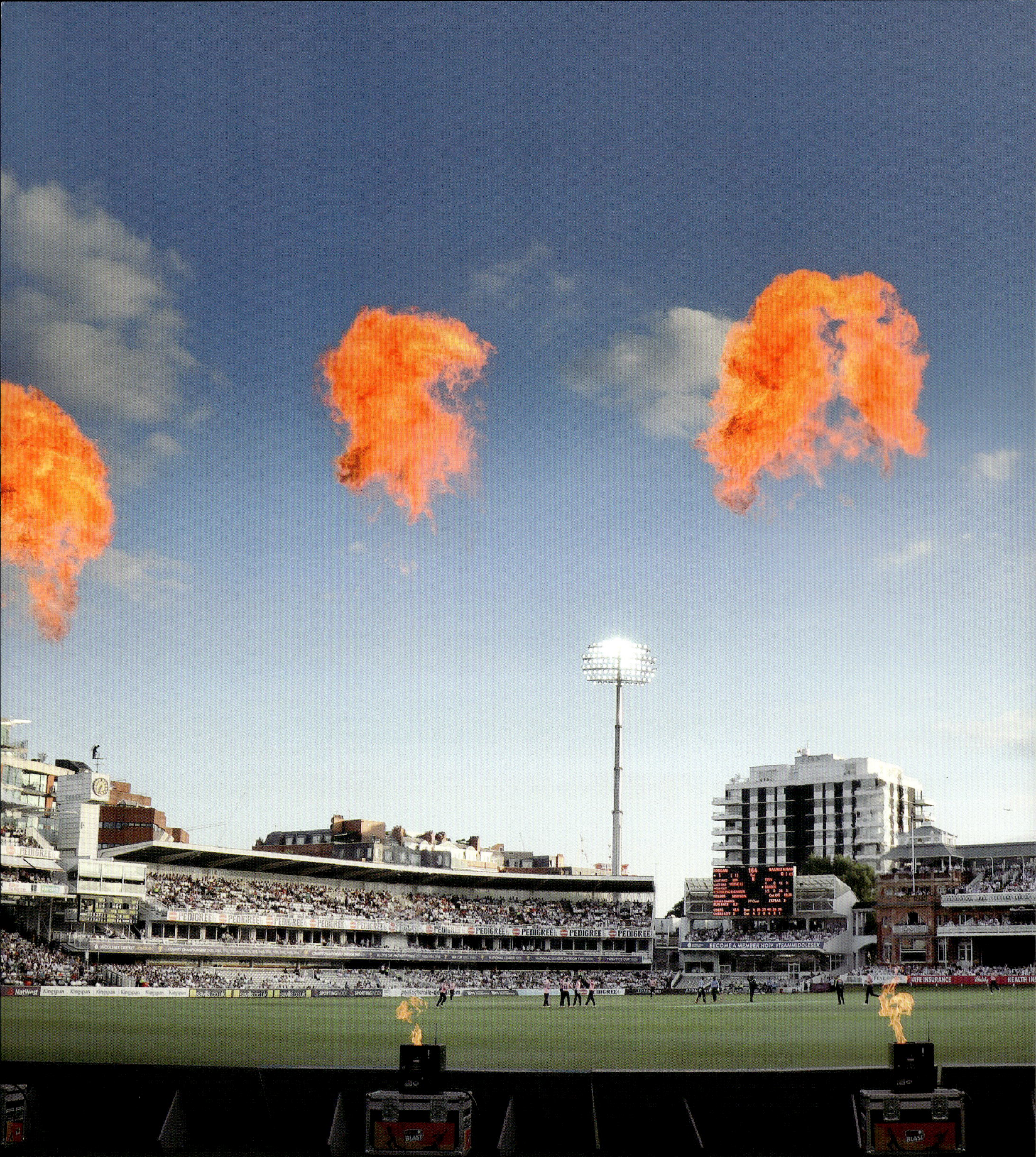

Introduction

Welcome to Lord's, the Home of Cricket and of Marylebone Cricket Club (MCC).

This short guide is intended to complement your visit to Lord's, whether as a spectator or as a visitor on one of the popular Lord's tours.

The following pages will lead you through the history and development of this most famous of all cricket grounds, exploring its outstanding architecture and introducing you to some of the characters who have made this such a special venue.

We hope that this guide will add to the enjoyment of your visit to the Home of Cricket and look forward to seeing you again soon.

Guy Lavender
Chief Executive & Secretary
Marylebone Cricket Club

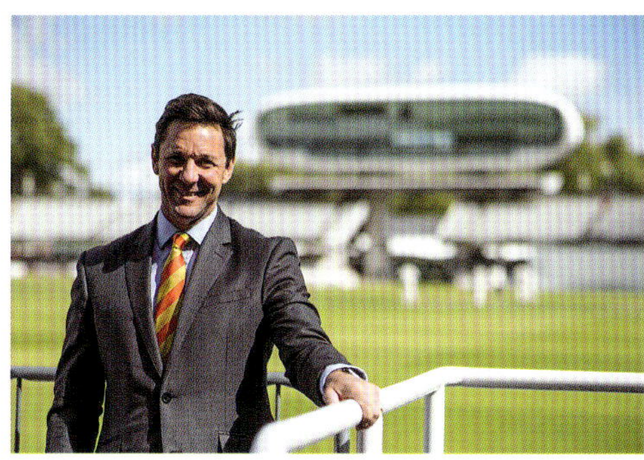

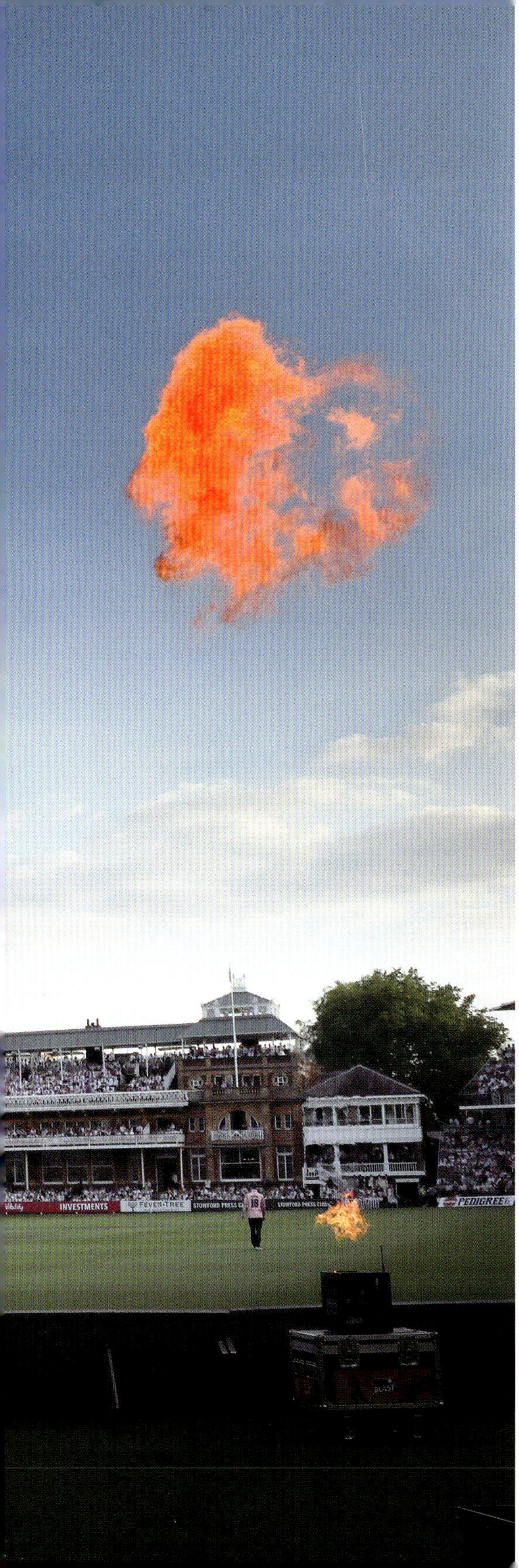

Pyrotechnics add to the spectacle for the crowd at a T20 Vitality Blast match between Middlesex and Sussex in 2018. Sussex went on to win by 12 runs.

'Lord's is the ground by which all others are measured. No other ground comes near to doing the little things that players and spectators really remember... It is a privilege to play here.'

Joe Root

A portrait of William Gilbert Grace (1848–1915), painted by Archibald Stuart-Wortley, 1890. The greatest cricketer of his generation, Grace revolutionised the technique of batting.

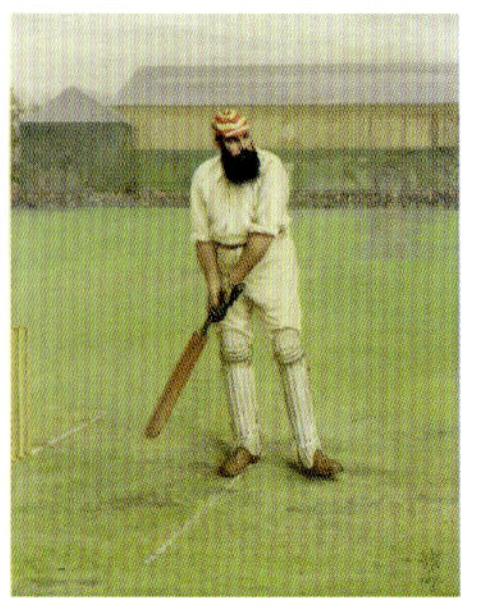

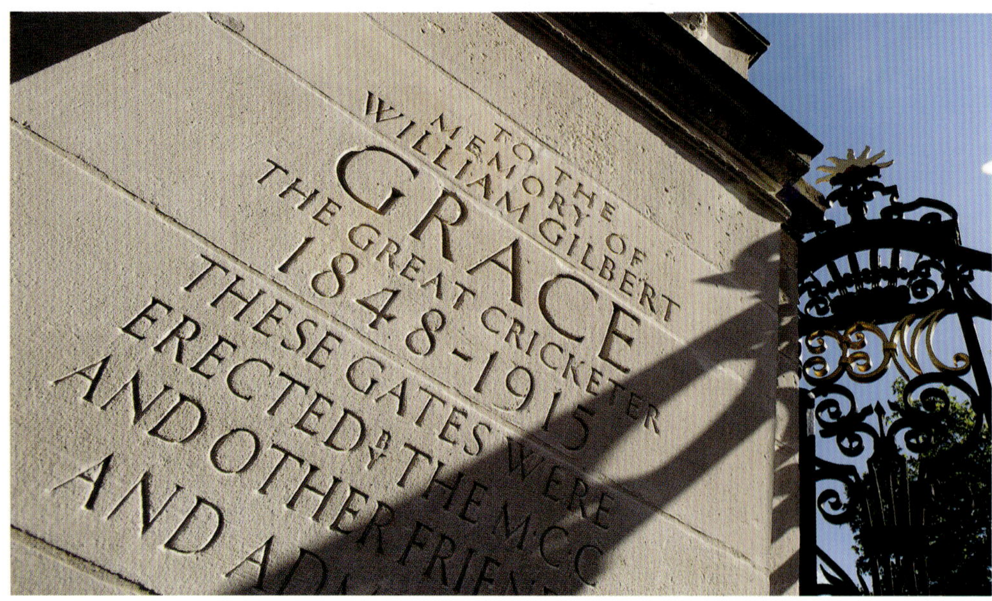

The Grace Gates

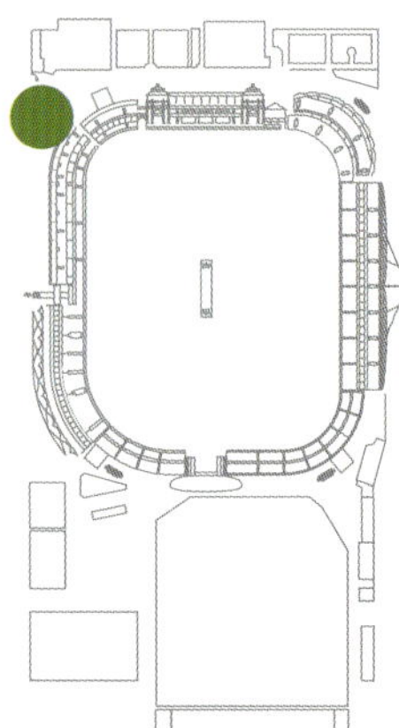

The W.G. Grace Gates traditionally welcome visitors to Lord's. Erected in 1923 by the Bromsgrove Guild, they were designed by MCC's architect Sir Herbert Baker as a memorial to the great cricketer. More than a century after his death, he remains instantly recognisable as one of the most famous of all cricketers.

William Gilbert Grace was one of five brothers (three of whom played cricket for England). He burst onto the cricket scene, making his first century aged only fifteen, and went on to dominate the game for almost 40 years. He attracted serious notice at Lord's in 1868, when he scored a brilliant century for the Gentlemen against the Players, and in 1871 he became the first cricketer ever to reach 2,000 runs in a season. In 1873 Grace was the first to achieve the double of 1,000 runs and 100 wickets in a season, a feat he achieved each year until 1878. He captained Gloucestershire for 25 years, twice leading the side to the County Championship, and played in 22 Test Matches against Australia, often as Captain. Among them was the first Test played in England in 1880, in which he scored the first Test century in England.

As well as being a great cricketer, Grace was a larger-than-life character, not averse to bending the Laws when it suited him. Many of the stories told about him refusing to walk when given out are true – he knew that people had come to see him bat!

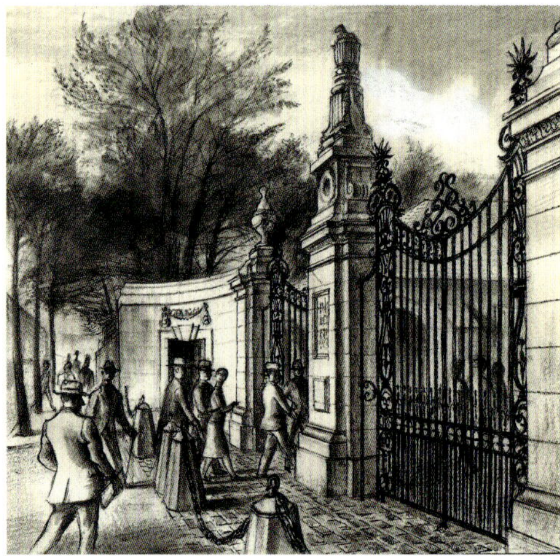

Sketch of the Grace Gates by an unknown artist, 1923. The construction of the new Tavern pub and banqueting suite in 1967 meant the gates had to be moved 13 feet from their original position.

The Coronation Garden

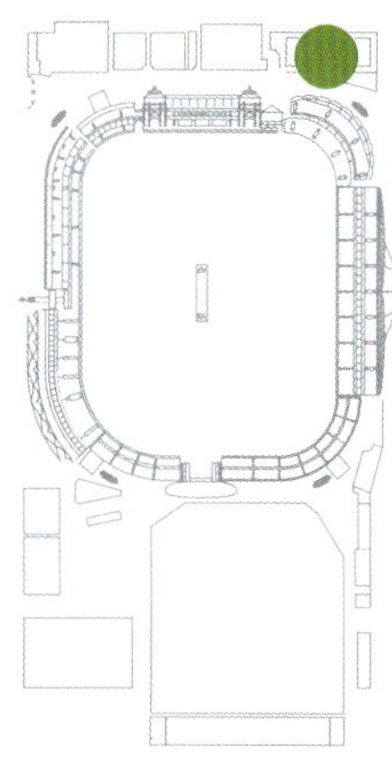

The Coronation Garden was laid out in 1953, the year of Elizabeth II's coronation, and is the most popular of picnic spots at Lord's. Before play begins, rugs and baskets are laid out on the grass. From lunchtime onwards parties of Members and friends can be found enjoying the leafy surroundings, as generations of cricket watchers have done before. Several benches are dedicated to famous players. Even some trees form memorials to cricketers past, most recently the eucalyptus dedicated to the great Australian all-rounder Keith Miller.

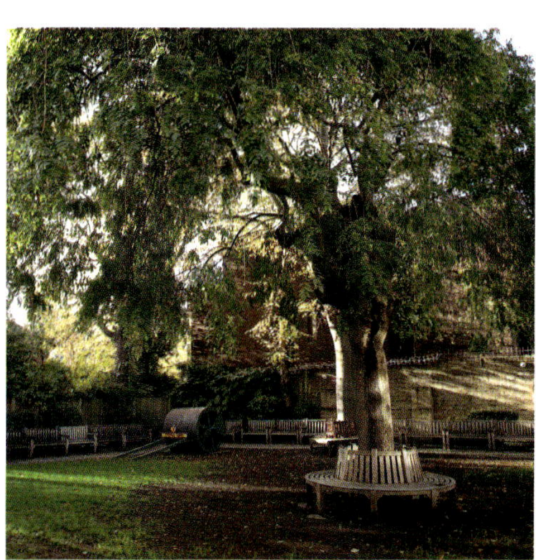

Below: Picnickers enjoying the Coronation Garden during the 2017 England v South Africa Test Match.

Right: The north-west corner of the Coronation Garden, with the Club's famous Thomas Lord roller in the background.

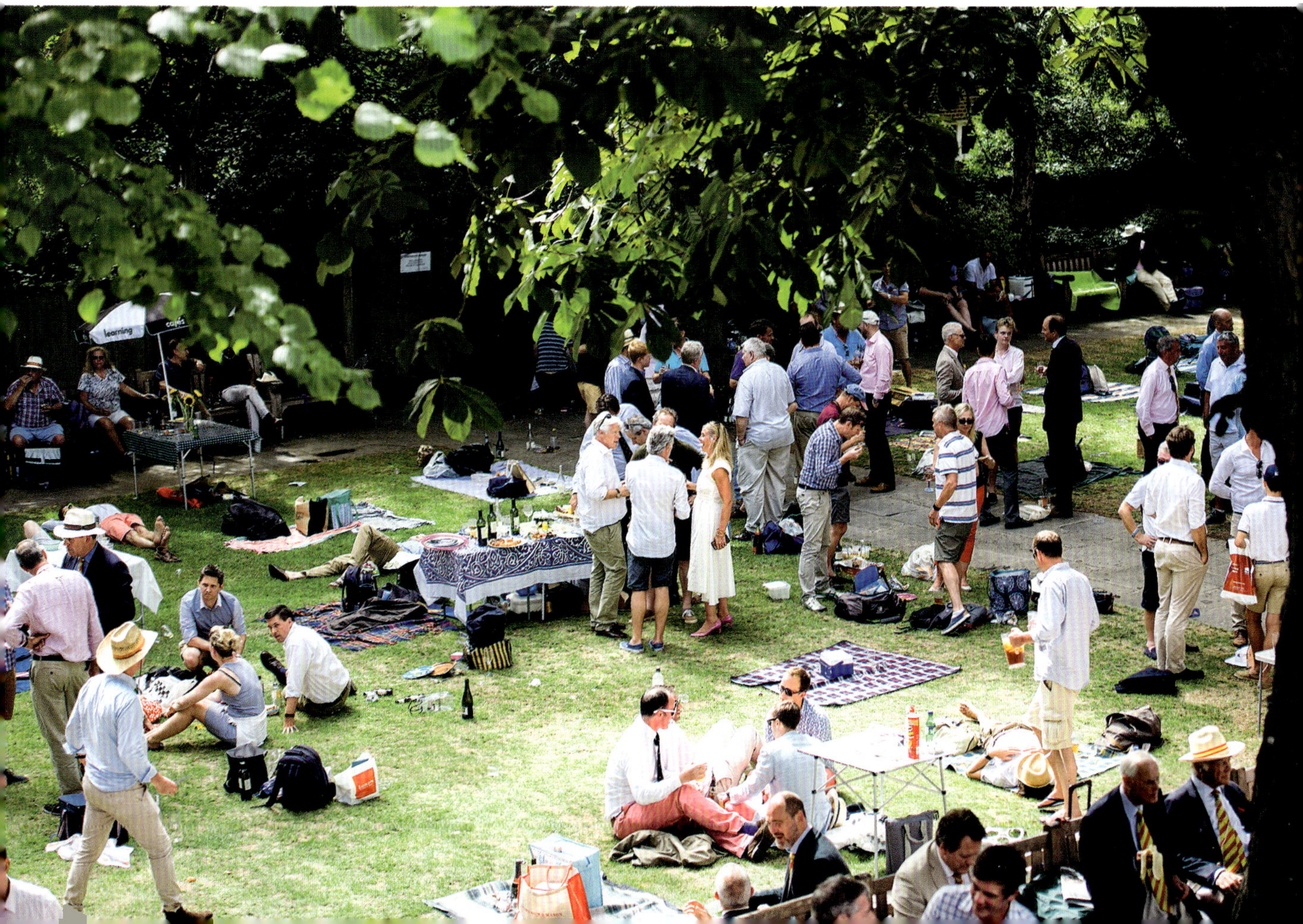

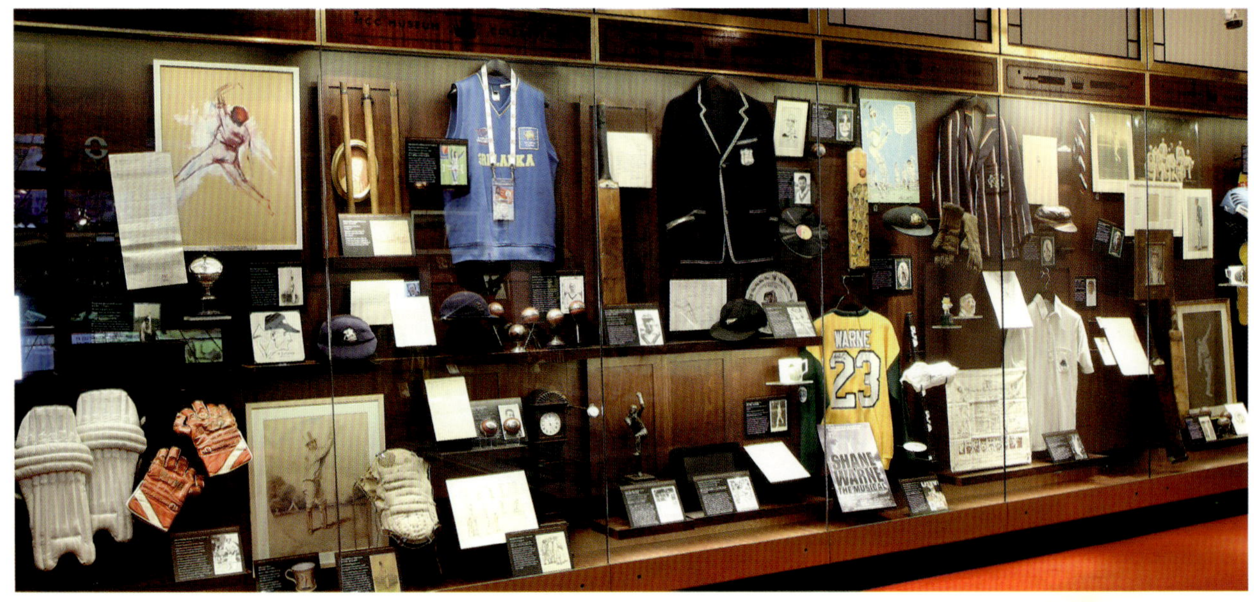

Museum, Library and Archive

In 1864 MCC owned only two pictures when its Treasurer, Sir Spencer Ponsonby- Fane, persuaded the Committee to enhance the appearance of the Pavilion. At the latest count the Club's collection – the biggest in the world dedicated to cricket – numbers around 80,000 items. These are housed primarily in the Archive, Library and Museum.

Originally opened in 1953 by HRH the Duke of Edinburgh and the Bishop of London, the Museum was known as the Imperial Cricket Memorial Gallery. It was dedicated to those cricketers all around the globe who had given their lives in wartime.

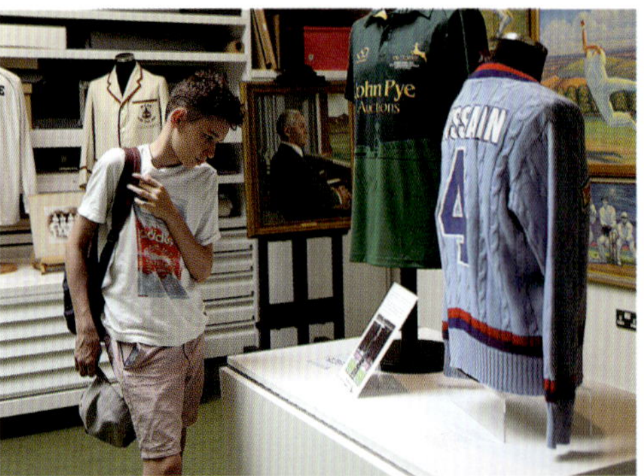

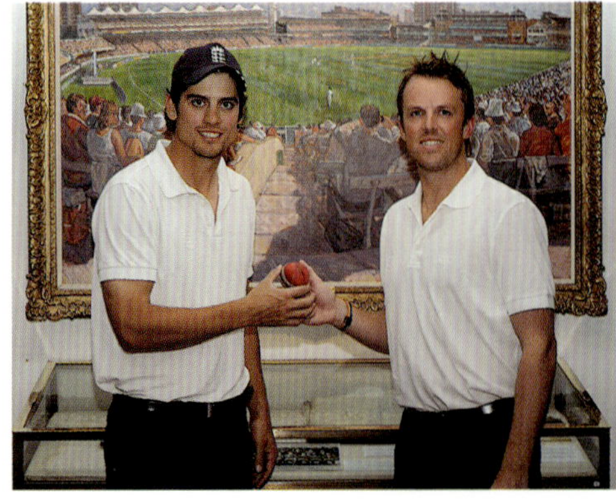

Above: Displays on the ground floor of the MCC Museum celebrate many of the great cricketers through the history of the game.

Above right: On major match days the Museum's upstairs workroom is sometimes opened to visitors.

Right: Sir Alastair Cook and Graeme Swann present the 2009 Ashes winning ball to the MCC Museum. Cook took the last catch of the Ashes Series to dismiss Michael Hussey of Australia from the bowling of Graeme Swann, sealing England's series win at The Oval.

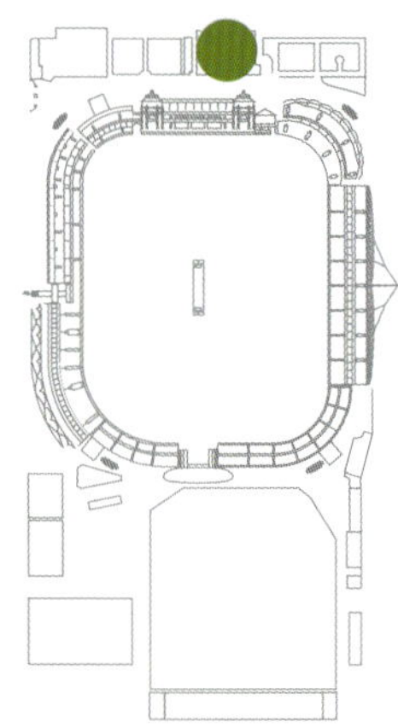

'The Lord's Library has been spectacularly renovated, revealing a treasure trove of information for any cricket enthusiast.'

Peter Oborne, *Wounded Tiger* (Simon & Schuster, 2014)

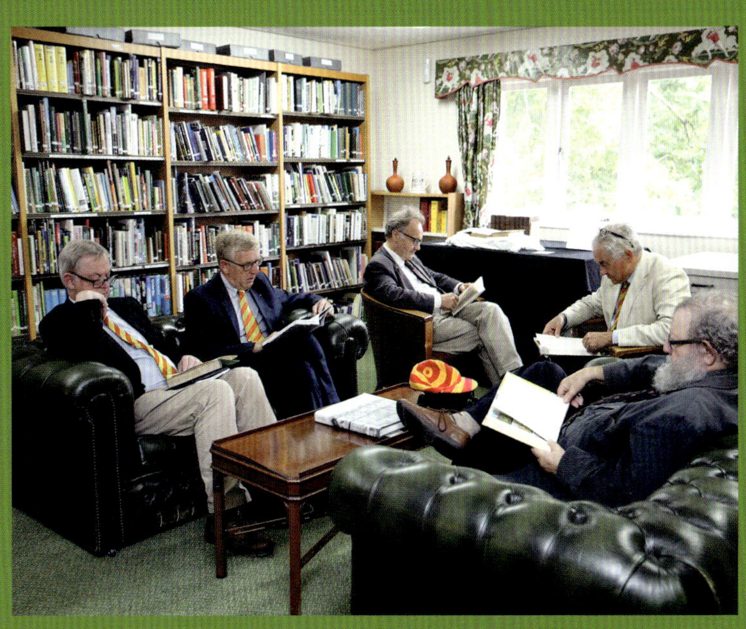

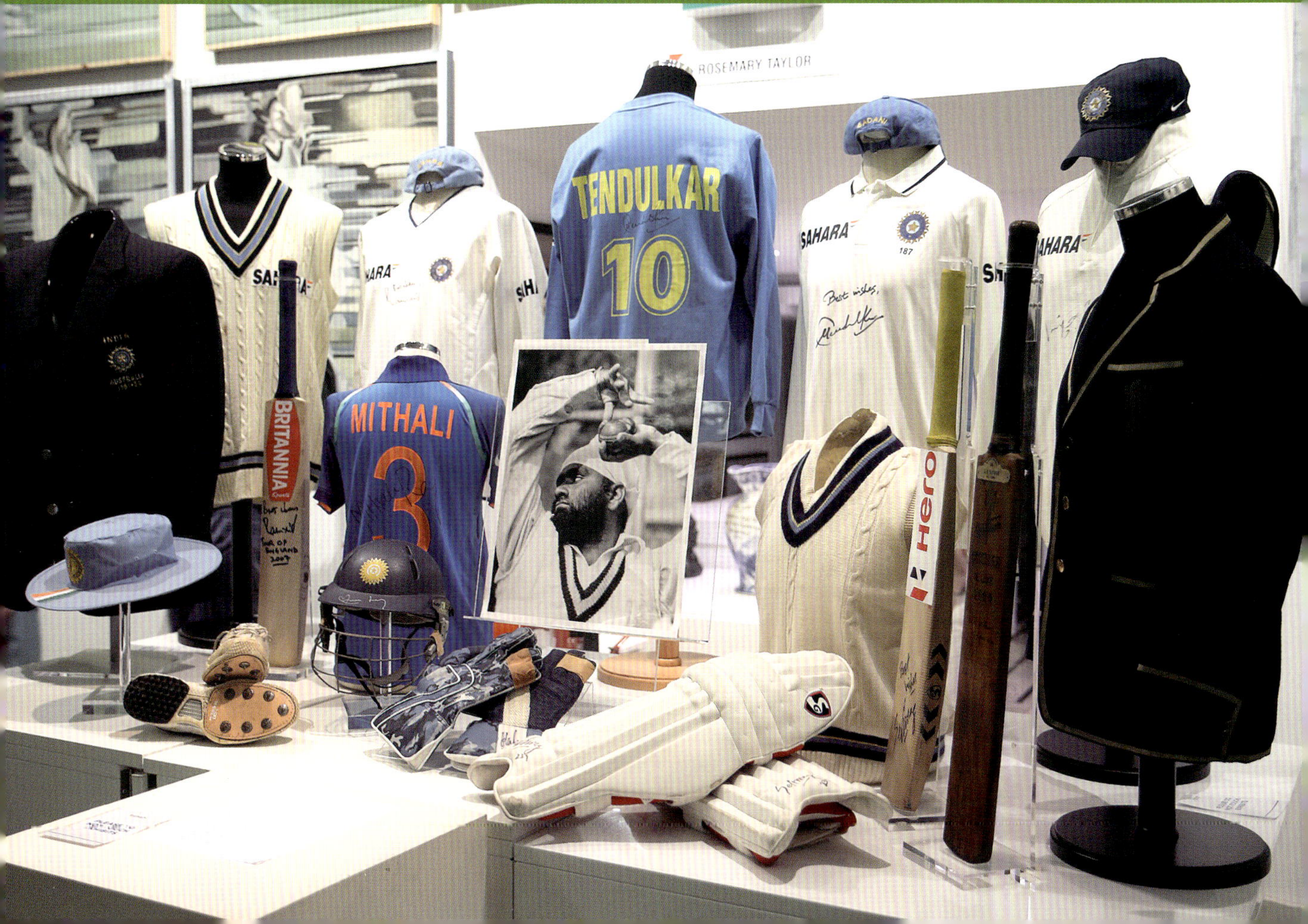

'Lord's must be a bit like Heaven.
There are many mansions in it.
It caters for all tastes, classes,
colours, ages, points of view,
degrees of skill, levels of
knowledge.'

T.C. Dodds, *Hit Hard and Enjoy it* (*The Cricketer*, 1976)

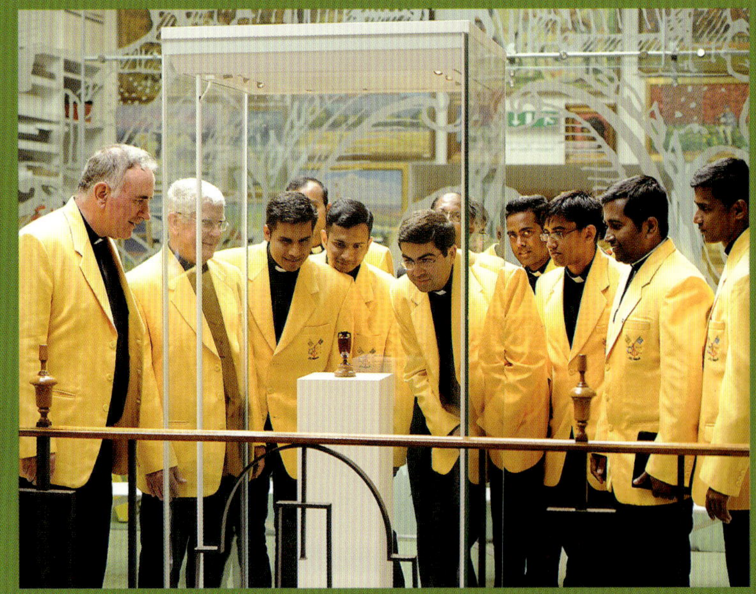

Below: The Ashes Urn, an icon of Anglo-Australian cricketing rivalry, remains the most famous object in the MCC Museum.

Right: Members of the Vatican cricket team visiting the Museum in 2016.

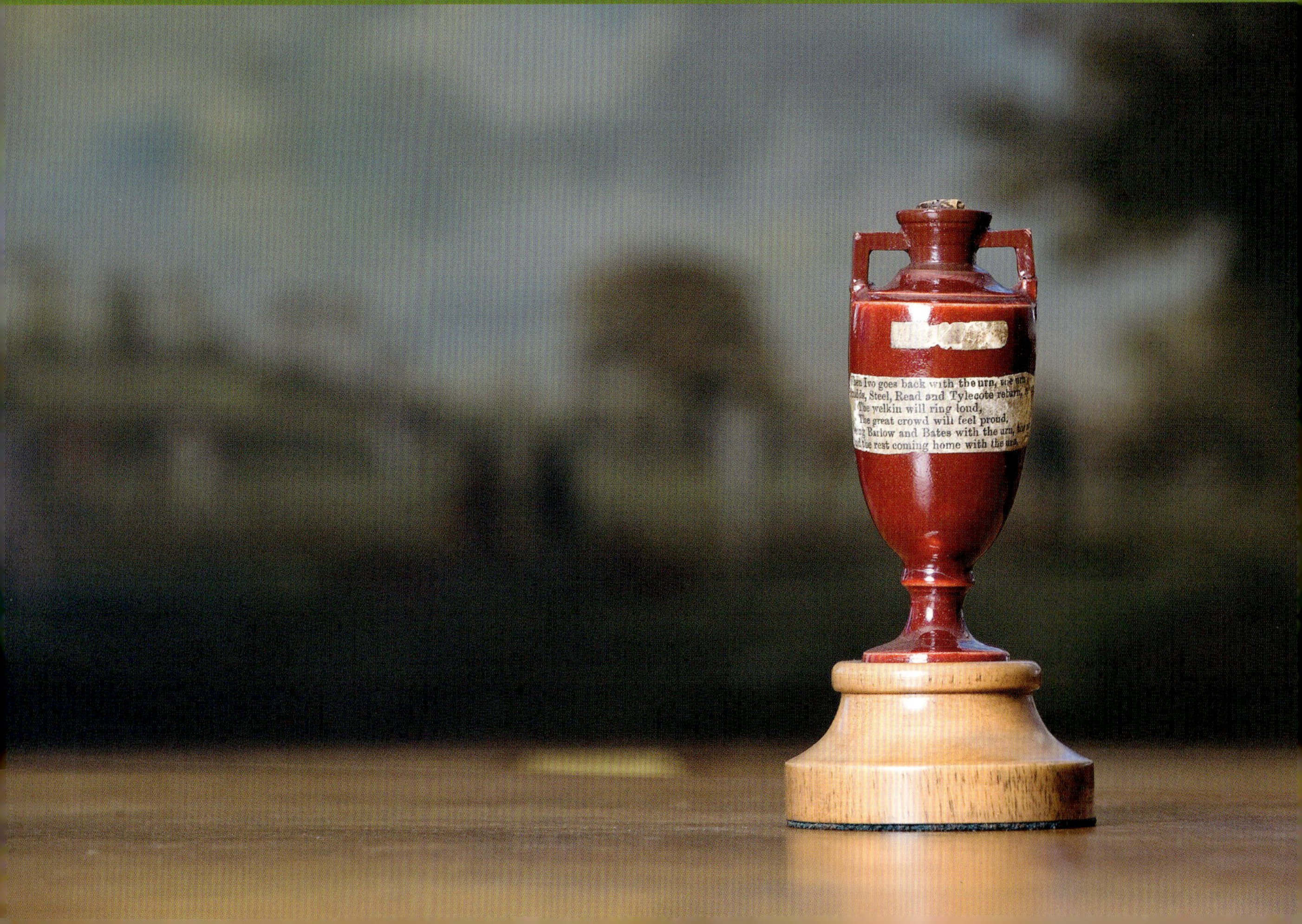

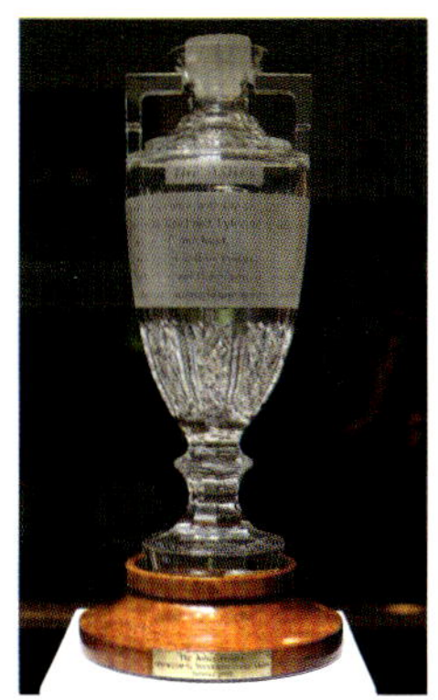

The MCC Waterford Crystal Ashes Trophy, the first official trophy for an Ashes Series, was commissioned by MCC. It has been presented to the victor of every Ashes Series since 1998–9.

Below: A Lord's Tour Guide gives a presentation to visitors in the Long Room during the 2018 MCC – Nepal – Netherlands Twenty20 tournament.

Below right: Silver mounted Emu Egg, presented to Mr W. Burrup, who helped to manage the first English touring team to Australia in 1861–2.

The Museum is home, of course, to cricket's most famous artefact. The Ashes Urn, standing only 4in (11cm) high and made of terracotta, has come to be recognised as the ultimate symbol of sporting rivalry.

Its story begins in 1882 when England were defeated by Australia for the first time in one of the most dramatic Test Matches ever played. The loss was considered a national calamity and a mock obituary notice appeared in the *Sporting Times*.

A topical reference to the debate on the legality of cremation, this idea captured the public's imagination. England's captain, the Hon. Ivo Bligh, took up 'the challenge' for the return series; he set off for Australia vowing 'to recover the ashes'.

The idea persisted throughout the tour in Australia. At Christmas time, the team stayed as guests at the palatial home of Sir William and Lady Clarke, sponsors of the tour. Here England played a match against the estate staff. As victorious captain, Bligh was presented with a small urn containing the ashes of a bail by Lady Clarke and friends – a mock trophy to symbolise the ashes which he had come so far to regain. The team continued their tour, beating Australia in the Test Series. Bligh returned to England, treasuring the Urn as a precious personal gift.

Yet the association of ashes with cricket was rekindled when, in 1903–4, it fell to MCC to organise England tours to and from Australia. Pelham Warner, the captain of that tour, entitled his book – for reasons that are still not clear – *How We Recovered the Ashes*. From that time onwards, the term has been applied to every Test cricket series between England and Australia.

When Ivo Bligh died in 1927 it must therefore have seemed a natural gesture to bequeath the 'original' ashes to MCC. Gradually the image of the Urn too has become indelibly linked with the rivalry of the two great cricketing nations.

Australian domination in the late 1980s–90s gave rise to calls for the Urn to be used as a trophy. MCC declined, citing its history as a gift. However, following discussions with the respective cricket boards, the Club commissioned a large crystal replica for this purpose.

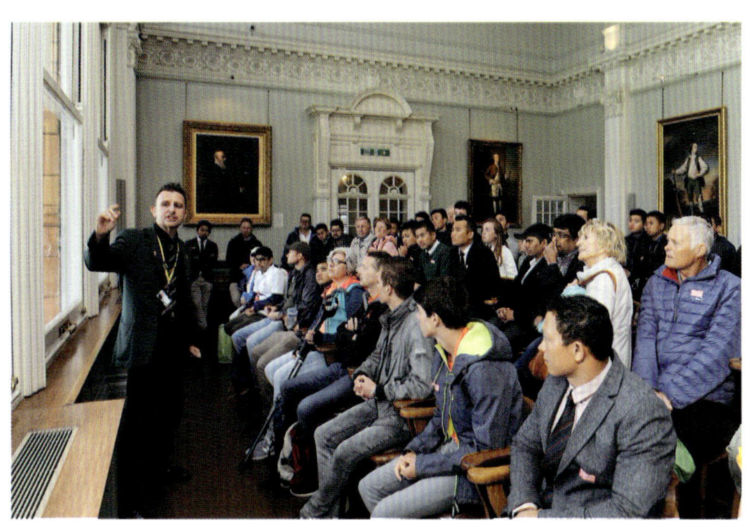

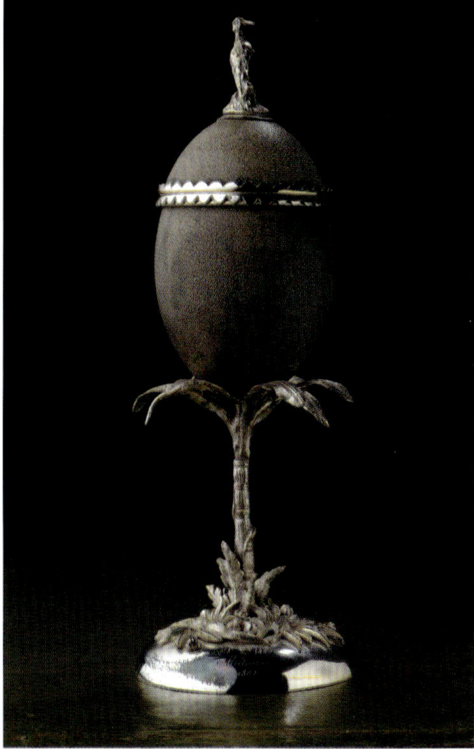

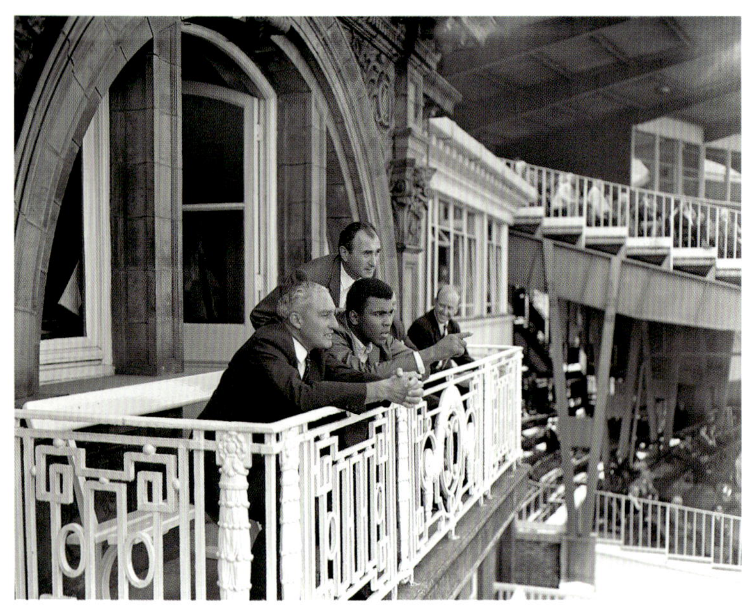

*'Really magnificent... the
building is apparently intended
to stand forever.'*

Bailey's Magazine, 1890

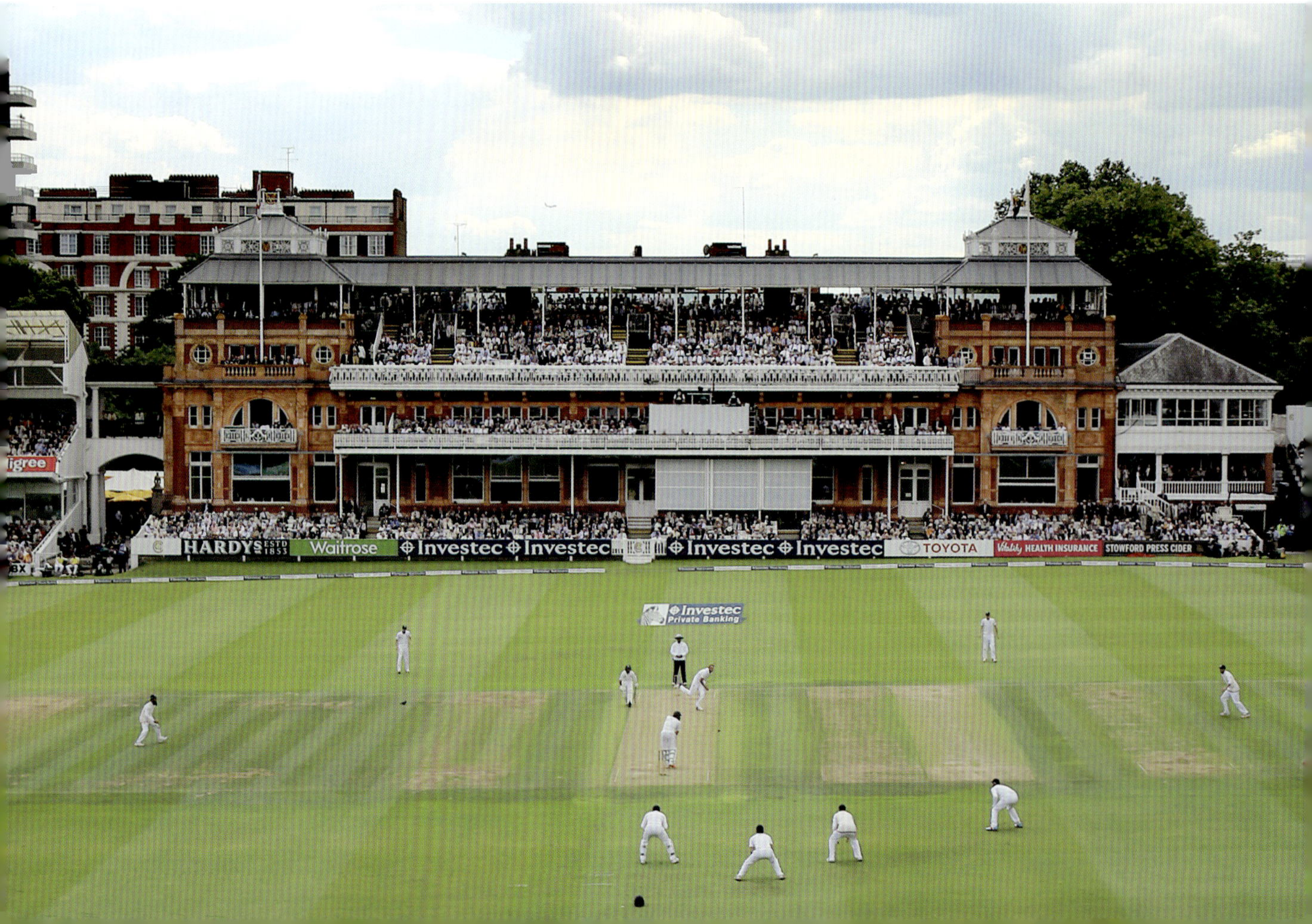

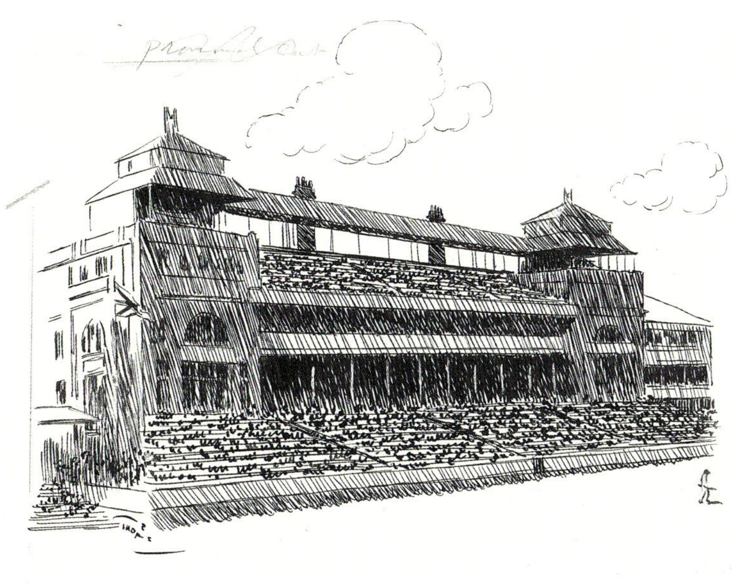

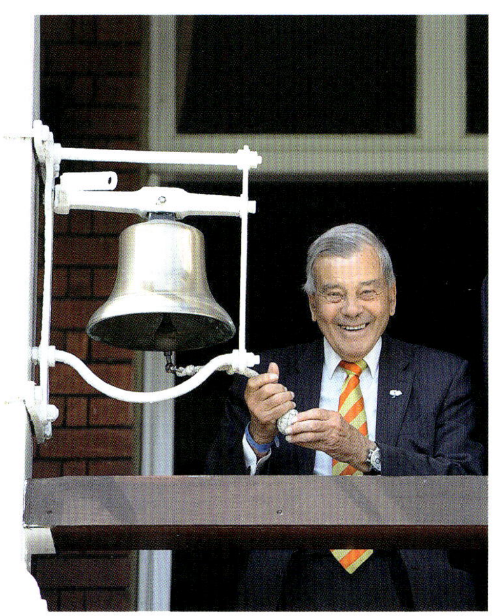

The Pavilion

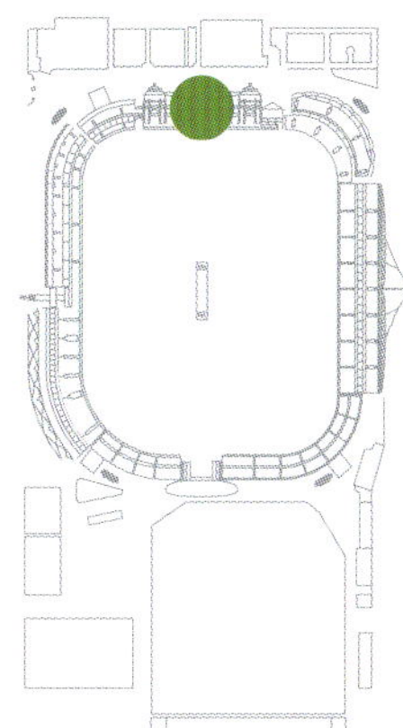

The Pavilion at Lord's is one of the most celebrated buildings in the sporting world; it received special Grade II* listed status from English Heritage in 1982. Designed by the architect Thomas Verity, it was constructed in the winter of 1889–90 at a cost of £21,000 (around £1.7 million in today's money) to serve an increased membership of 4,000.

During the winter of 2004–5 the Pavilion underwent its first major refurbishment since that time. The intention was to restore and conserve the building's important original features while also providing much improved facilities for players, staff, public and a membership that in 2018 numbered some 23,000.

The Pavilion is unusual in having had an extension added by the time it opened. The small building on its north side began as a single storey which, according to *Bailey's Magazine* in May 1890, was 'very much of the same pattern as the well-remembered rustic Pavilion'. It was used as a players' room by the professionals – not at that time permitted to use the same changing room facilities as their team-mates who were gentlemen amateurs.

The 'rustic pavilion' referred to the current Pavilion's predecessor, erected in 1826 following a fire which destroyed the original clubhouse after the Eton v Harrow match of 1825. The second pavilion went through many alterations and extensions during its lifetime. It was eventually dismantled and reassembled on a private estate in Sussex.

Above left: *The Majesty of Empire: Headley Leaving Lord's Pavilion*. Sketch by James Thorpe, 1933.

Above right: Former international umpire Harold 'Dickie' Bird ringing the five-minute bell in 2015.

Thomas Lord

Lord was an ambitious Yorkshireman who had come to London to build a business in the wine trade. An astute businessman and capable cricketer, he was quick to seize the opportunity presented to him by the noblemen of the White Conduit Club, for whom he worked as a ground bowler and attendant.

One of the leading London clubs, the WCC was based in Islington. Some of its aristocratic members sought a more central location, however, and asked Lord to arrange it. In 1787 he obtained a lease on an area then known as Dorset Fields. Here he erected a high wooden fence, built a hut for cricketers to store their equipment and situated his wine shop at the entrance.

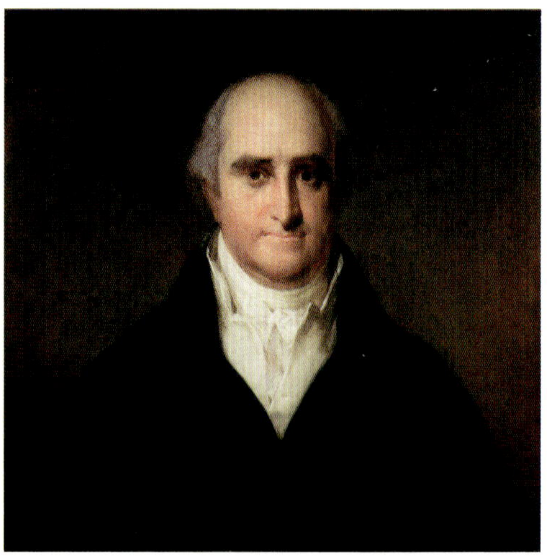

Thomas Lord's ground proved popular with the members, who were soon calling themselves the Marylebone Club in reference to their new district. However, with London expanding and rents rising rapidly, Lord was soon forced to make other plans. A move in 1811 to another site proved short-lived when the following year Parliament announced the route of the new Regent's Canal would cut right through it. But Lord managed to turn circumstance to his advantage. In 1814 he settled on the current site, achieving both a reduced rent and a significant compensation package.

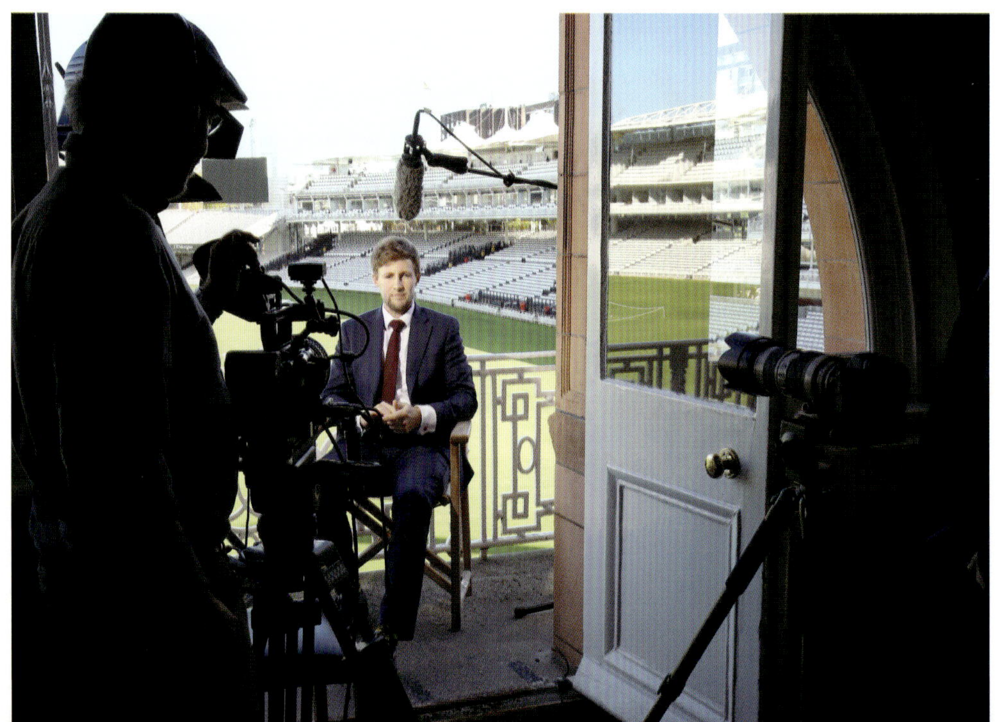

Above: A portrait of Thomas Lord (1755–1832) by an unknown artist, c.1830.

Left: Joe Root gives a television interview on the balcony of the home Dressing Room prior to England's tour of Australia in 2017–18.

Despite the popularity of cricket, Lord became increasingly unhappy with the profits he was making. Now aged almost 70, he planned one last business speculation. In 1823 he shocked MCC by announcing that he had permission to develop houses on the site – leaving only 150 square yards for cricket.

MCC was saved by one of its Members, William Ward. A director of the Bank of England and MP for the City of London, Ward was particularly fond of Lord's. In 1820 he had made a record innings of 278 at the Ground – a record that survived almost a century. Horrified by the proposal, he wrote Lord a cheque for £5,400 and thus retained the Ground for MCC.

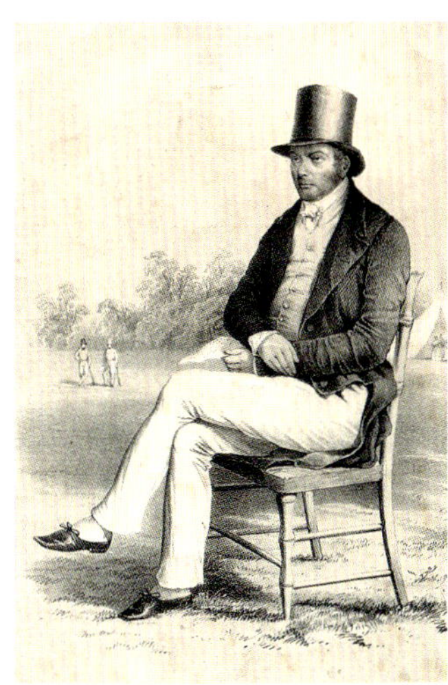

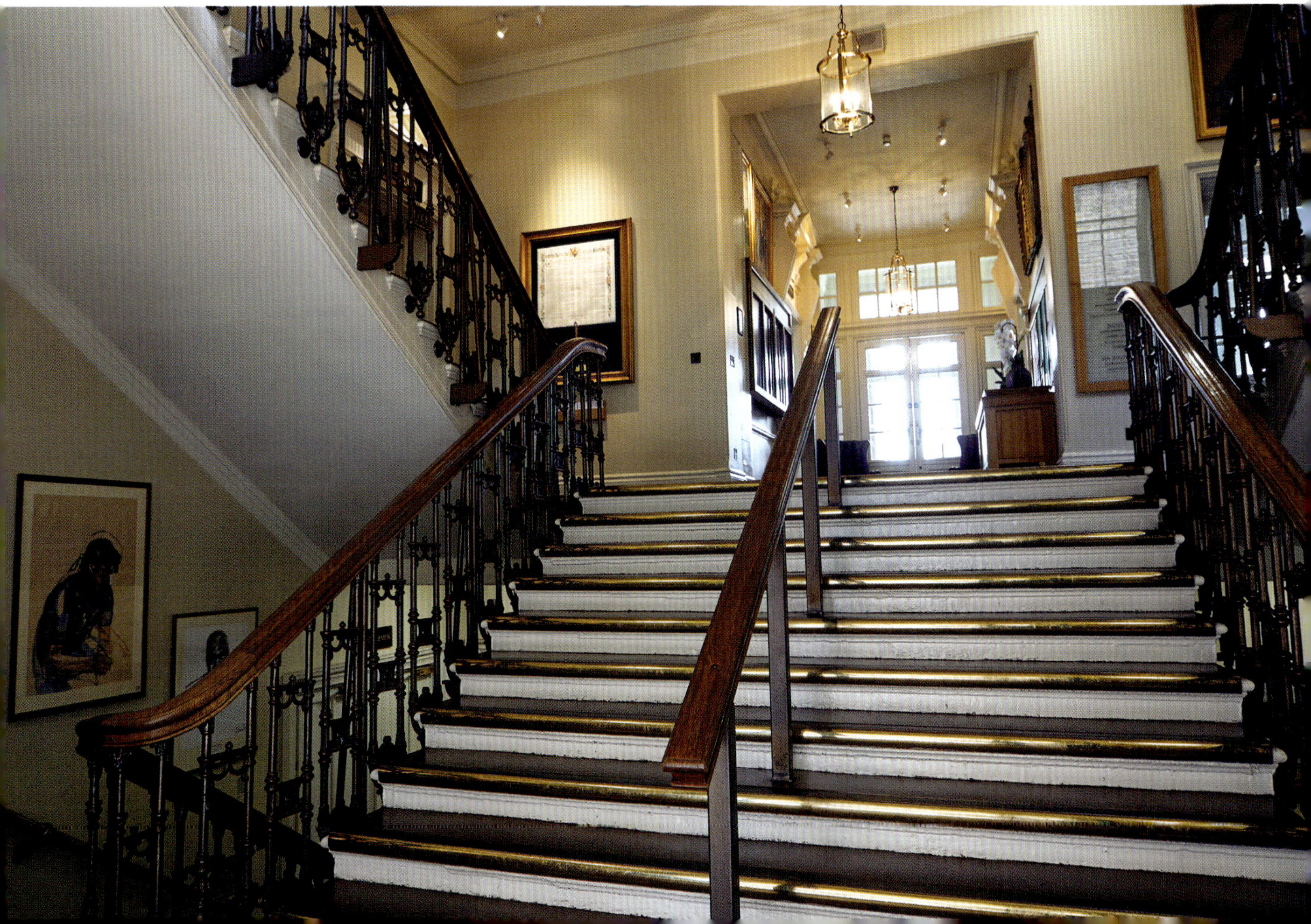

Right: A portrait of William Ward (1787–1849). This print was published by W.H. Mason in 1849 after an original drawing by William Drummond.

Below: The impressive north staircase leads from the main Pavilion entrance to the Long Room, Writing Room and Old Library. The Pavilion is the third to stand on the site and was opened in May 1890.

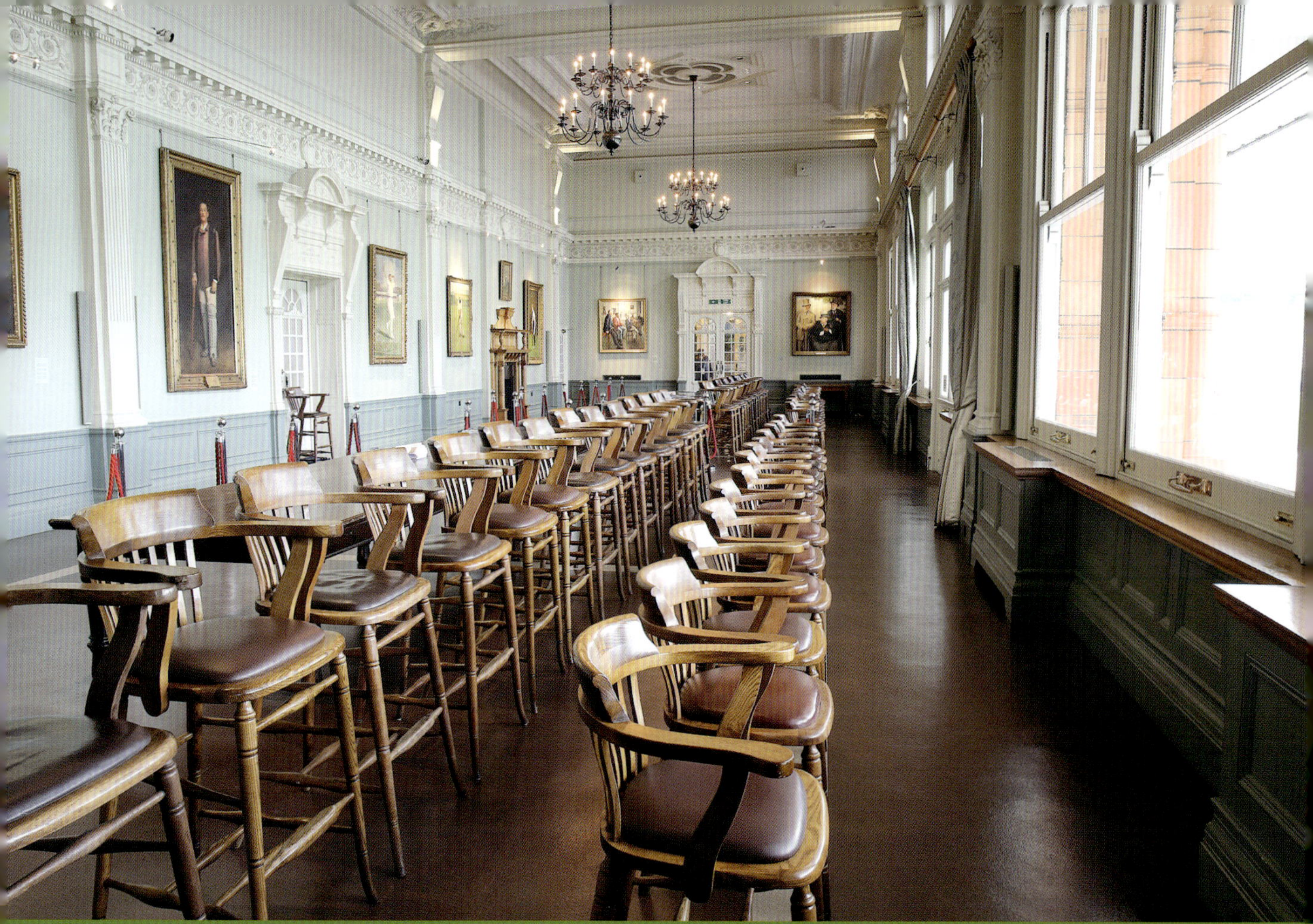

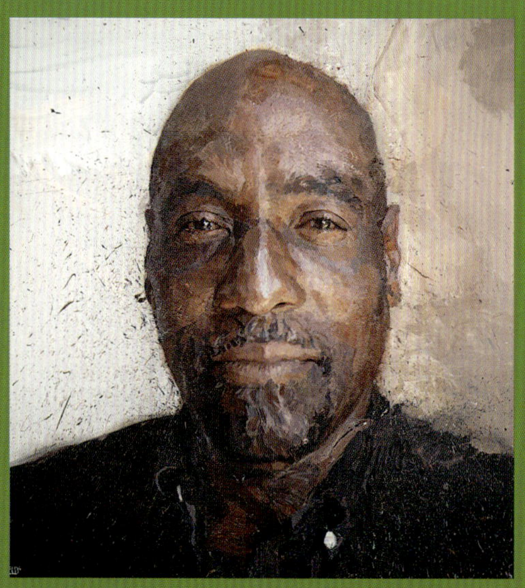

Left: *Portrait of Sir Vivian Richards* by Brendan Kelly, 2006. MCC has commissioned portraits of many great cricketers of recent years, such as Kumar Sangakkara, Kapil Dev and Brian Lara.

Above: The Long Room set up for a match day. MCC Members often queue from the early hours of the morning to secure the best seats on a major match day.

'Each time I've been back to Lord's I make a point of walking out onto the pitch, down the halls and through the players' rooms, soaking in all of the history and tradition. It always sends tingles down my spine.'

Former Australian cricketer Glenn McGrath, quoted in *A Portrait of Lord's*, A. Chadwick (Scala, 2013), p.127

The Long Room

For most cricket enthusiasts the highlight of the Lord's Tour is a visit to the famous Long Room that forms the heart of the Pavilion. Its name harks back to the 'Long Rooms' offering food and wine that formed the centrepiece of the 18th-century pleasure grounds beside which cricket was originally played in London.

Measuring 90 ft (27 m) in length, the Long Room also resembles the picture galleries of the nation's great stately homes. These provided not only a showcase for family portraits and treasures, but also a significant space for the indoor exercise and entertainment often required by the inclement British weather.

Middlesex Women walking out through the Long Room before their match against MCC Women, April 2018.

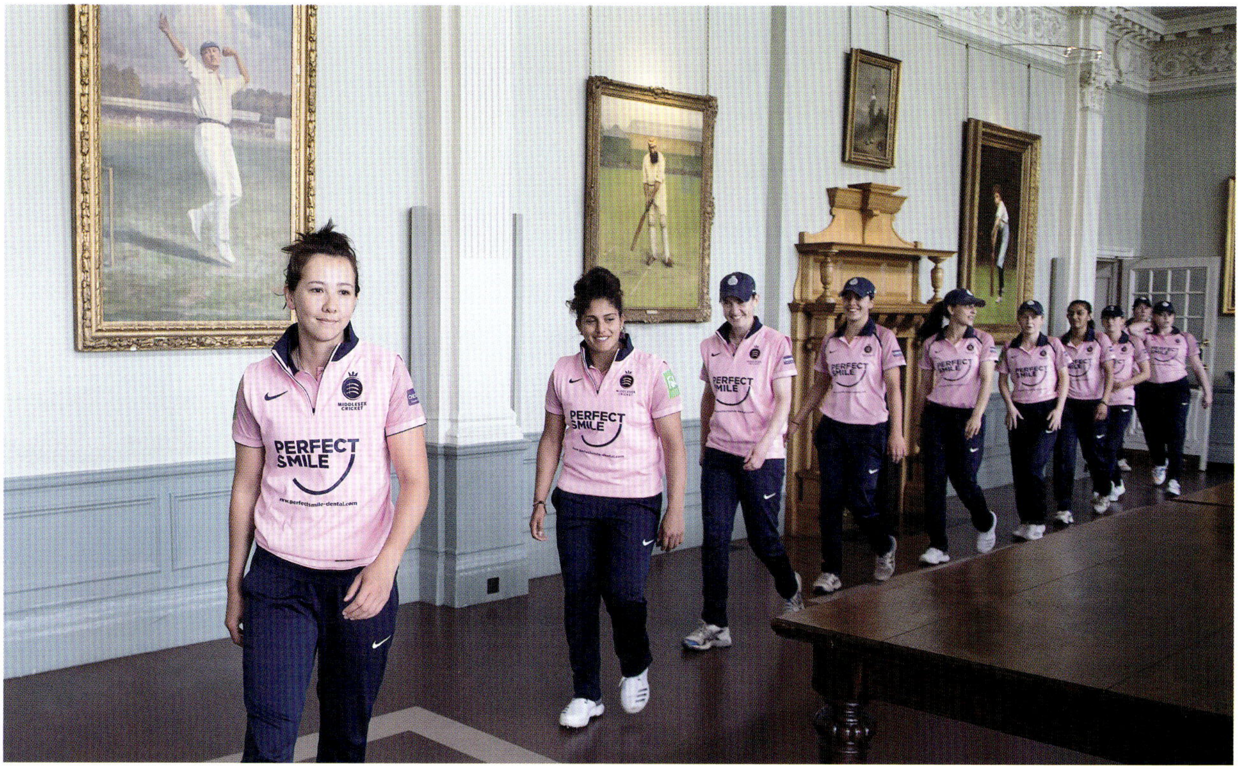

The finest of MCC's pictures spanning the entire history of cricket have continuously lined the walls, excepting only the war years. They form a stunning backdrop for Club dinners and events – as well as for players on match days. Both teams make their entrance on to the field through this very room.

Lord's is the only Test Ground where players walk through 'spectators' to the pitch, the spectators in this case being MCC Members. On the big Test Match days between five and six hundred Members often wait to greet the players emerging from their respective dressing rooms. A huge buzz of excitement arises – exacerbated by the acoustics – as the teams make their way out through the Long Room before the start of play.

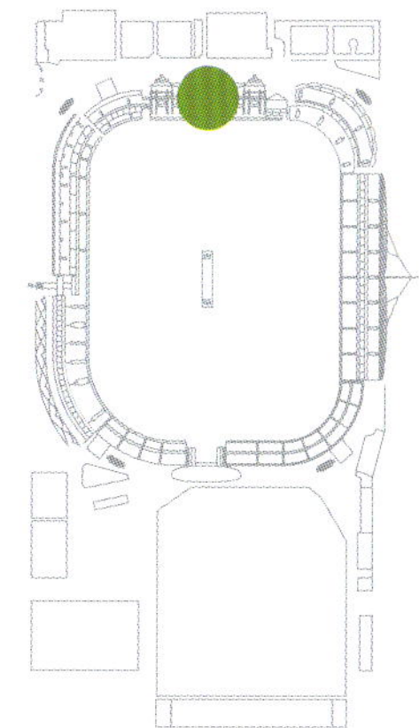

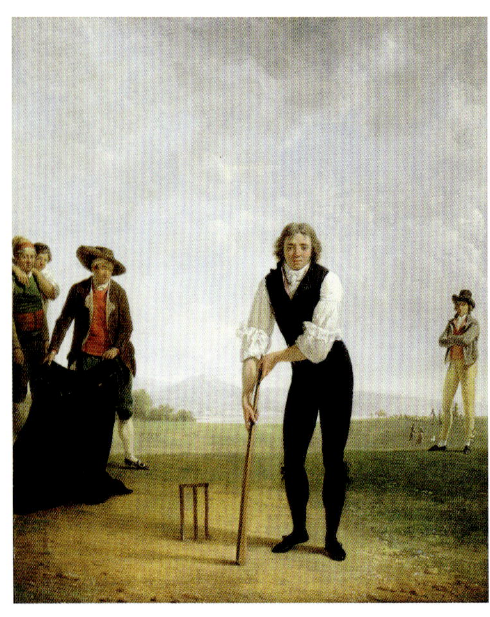

Left: *Thomas Hope of Amsterdam Playing Cricket with his Friends* by Jacques Sablet, 1792. This famous painting shows a wealthy young Englishman on the 'grand tour'; the impromptu game of cricket takes place on the plains of southern Italy with Mount Vesuvius behind.

Below: During the winter the Long Room is often busy with dinners, lunches and many other events such as the annual Christmas carol concert in aid of St. John's Hospice.

Members do not have assigned seats in the Pavilion. Many queue from the early hours of the morning until the gates open. A rush then begins by those keen to secure the best viewing positions, including the traditional 'high' seats of the Long Room.

The enormous sash windows were not an original feature when the Pavilion was first built, but were introduced to improve views of the pitch. Fortunately there have been few occasions such as that in August 1945, when a straight six hit by Wally Hammond flew through the open doors and into the Long Room.

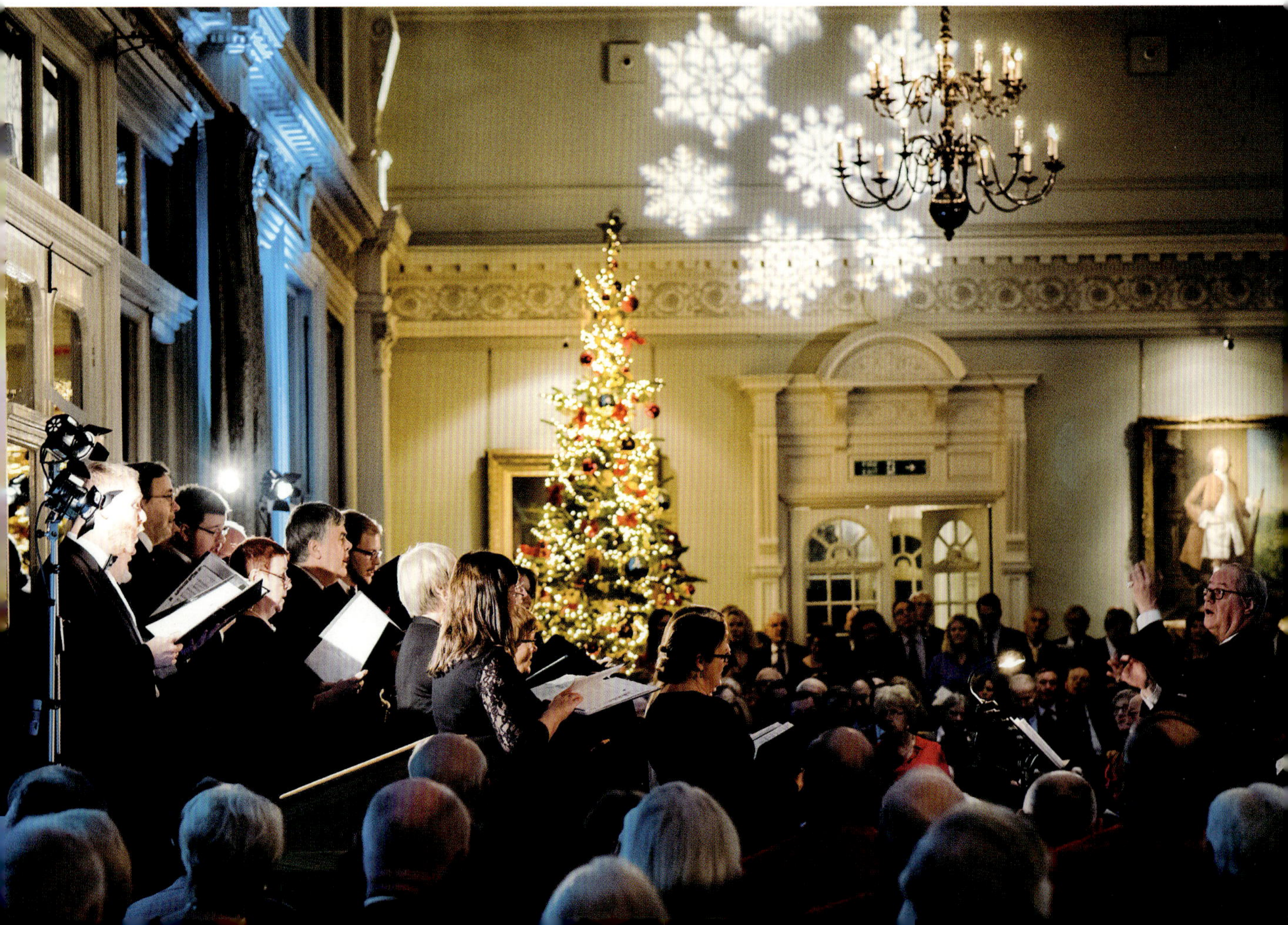

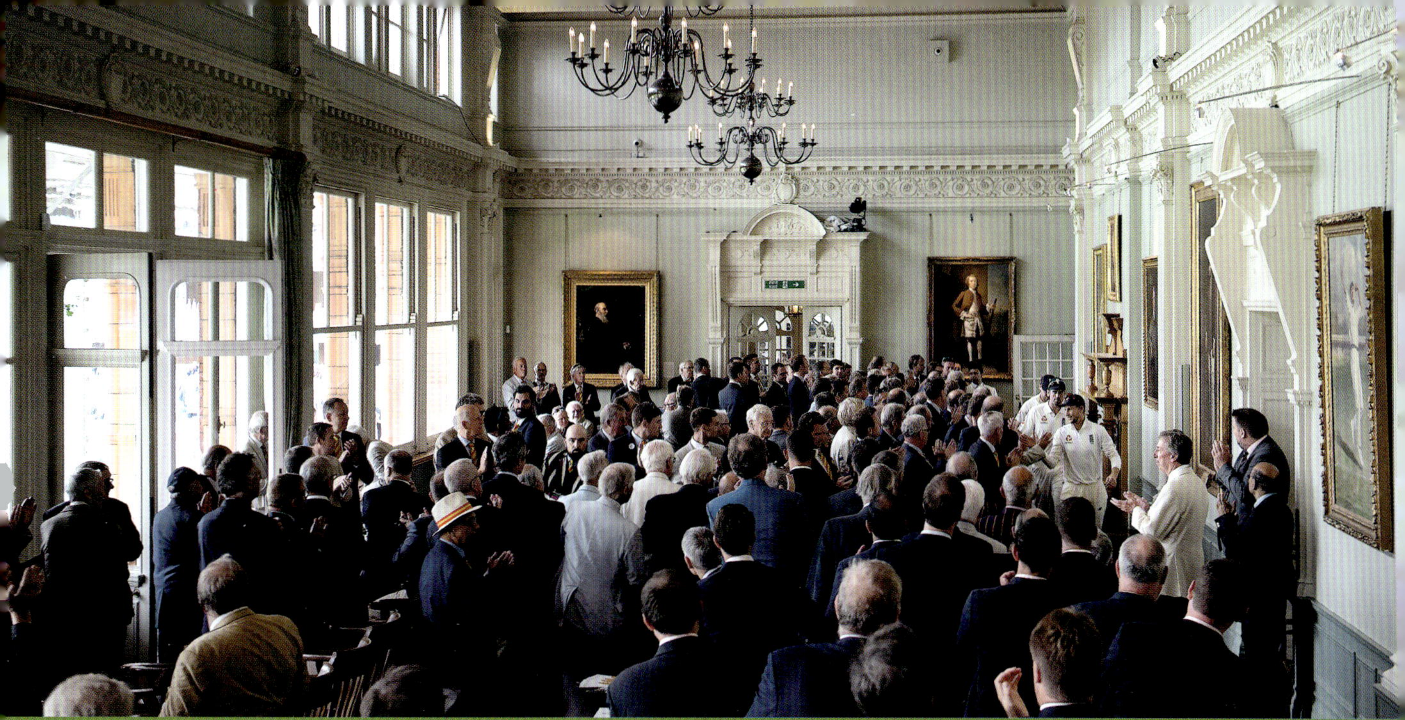

Above: Joe Root leads the England team out through the Long Room before taking the field against India in the 2018 Test Match.

Right: *The Young Cricketer: Portrait of Lewis Cage* by Francis Cotes RA, 1768. One of the finest examples of 18th-century cricketing art, this painting was purchased by MCC in 2008 and replaced a copy previously commissioned by the Club.

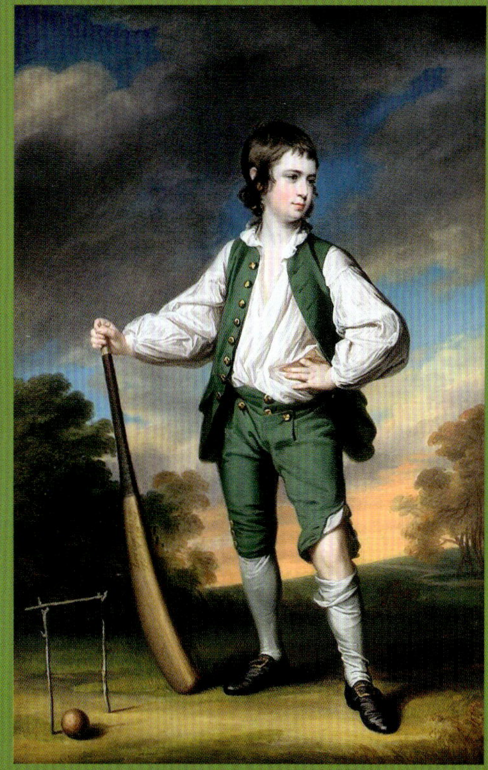

'There is nothing at all as splendid in its setting as the Pavilion at Lord's.'

Geoffrey Moorhouse, *Lord's* (Hodder & Stoughton, 1983). p.20

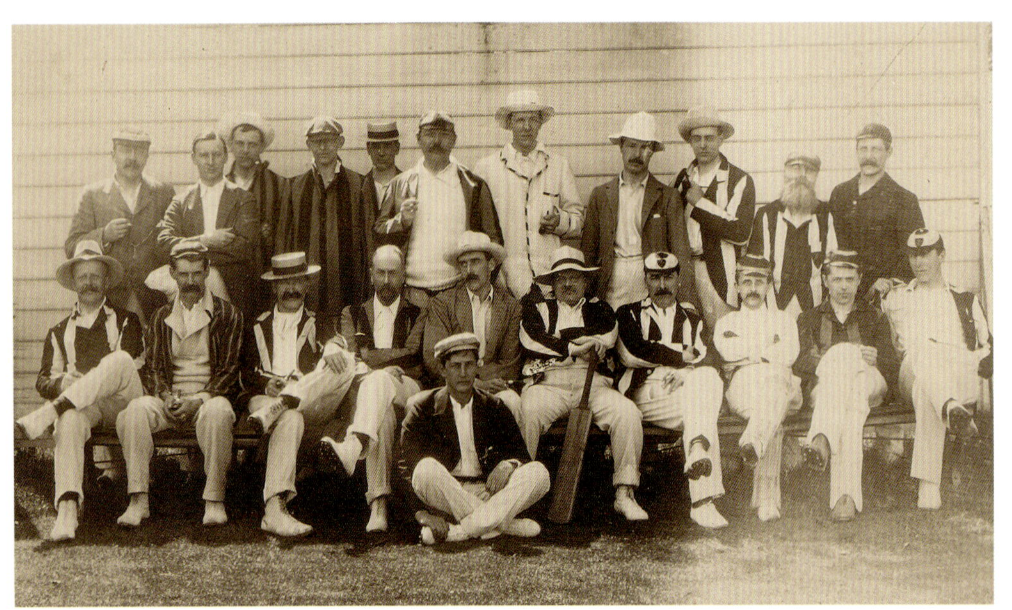

Left: Photograph of the teams from an Authors v Artists match in May 1903. Matches of this kind were a frequent occurrence at Lord's in the early 1900s. A regular player on the Authors' team was Sir Arthur Conan Doyle, author of the Sherlock Holmes stories, whose sole first-class wicket was that of W.G. Grace.

Below: The Writing Room is one of the most popular venues in the Pavilion, frequently being used for dinners, meetings, literary events and weddings.

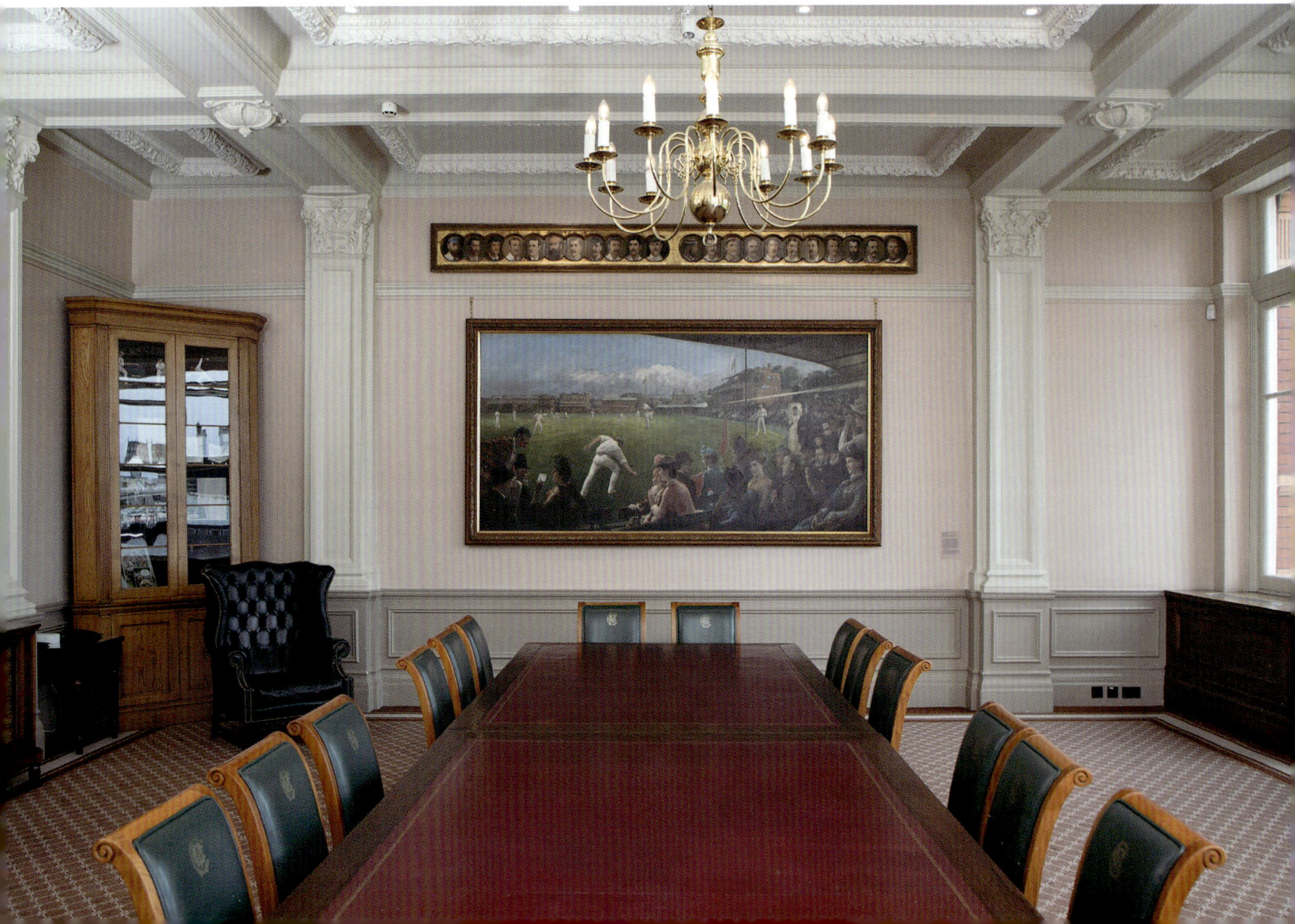

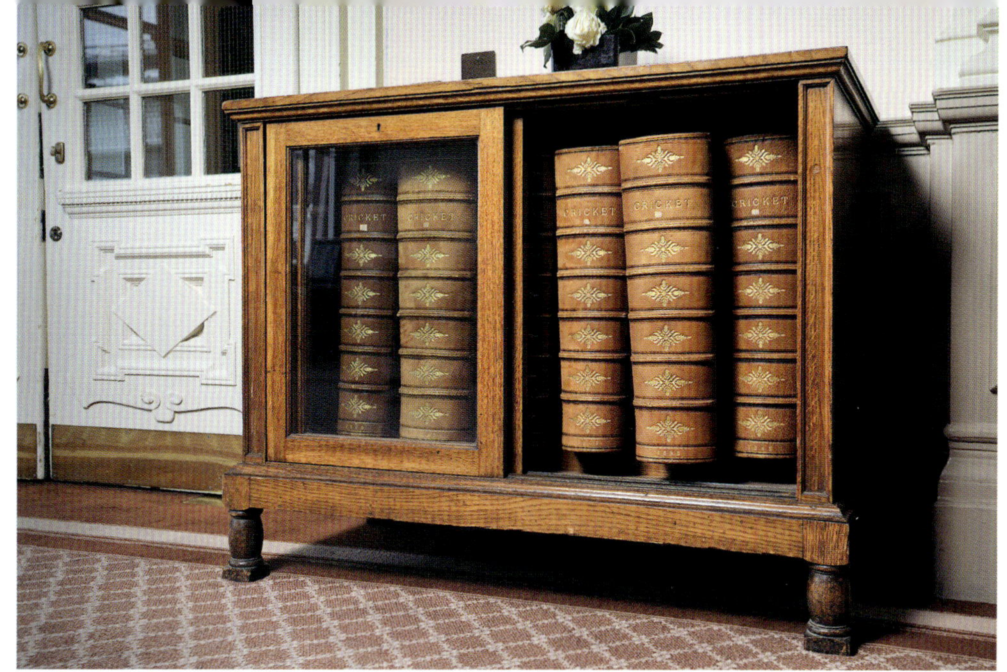

The Ford scrapbooks on display in the Writing Room. The 23 scrapbooks contain Alfred Lawson Ford's huge collection of early sketches, watercolours and other cricketing ephemera. They were donated to the MCC Library in 1930.

The Writing Room

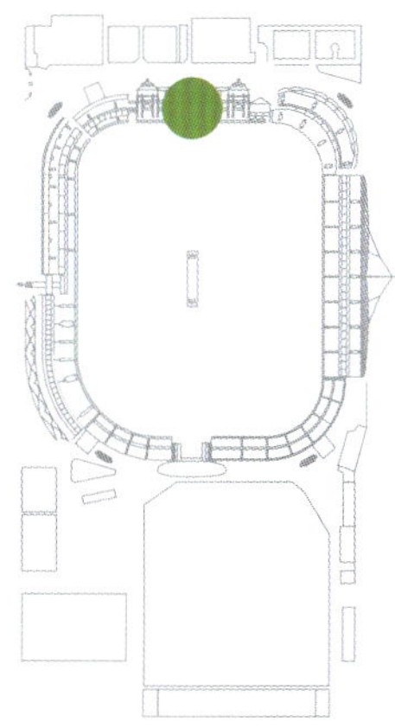

When the Pavilion first opened, the Writing Room was often used by Members wishing to conduct business while at Lord's. The room featured a mailbox and any letter posted to central London could be delivered by hansom cabs within the hour. For many years after this service was terminated, the Writing Room remained the Pavilion's quiet space. Here Members could read, write or study the cricket in comparative peace and quiet. On a match day, access to the Writing Room is restricted to MCC Members only.

Cricket has long enjoyed a reputation for inspiring the most enduring and respected literary culture in sport. In the 18th century it was the subject of epic poetry; by the early 19th century technical manuals on playing the game had begun to appear. By the middle of the 20th century hundreds of new cricket books were published each year, including mass-market tour books, popular annuals and player biographies.

The Writing Room today celebrates the depth and breadth of this literary culture. Its display cabinets feature items relating to some of the game's finest writers and broadcasters, as well as the massive, elephant folio scrapbooks of one of cricket's great collectors, Alfred Lawson Ford. In the corridor outside the room hang portraits of celebrated figures such as E.W. Swanton, C.L.R. James and Henry Blofeld.

E.W. Swanton's copy of the 1939 *Wisden*, which he kept while a Prisoner of War from 1942 to 1945.

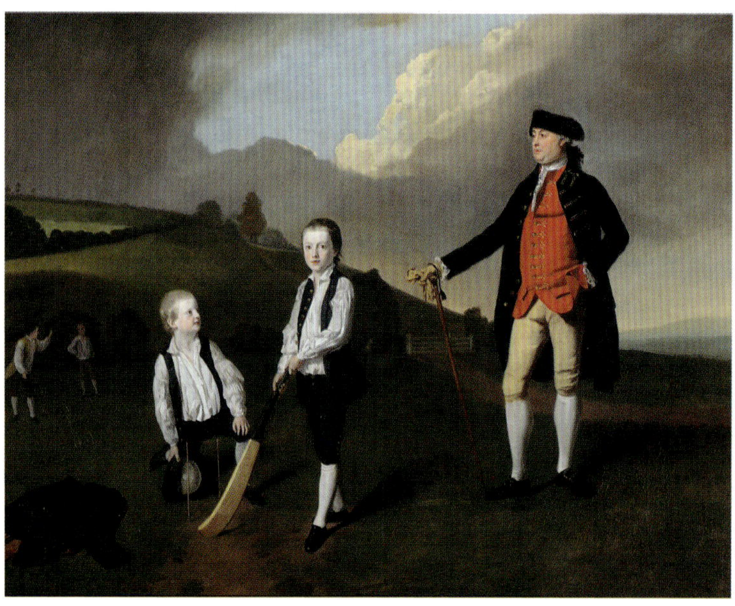

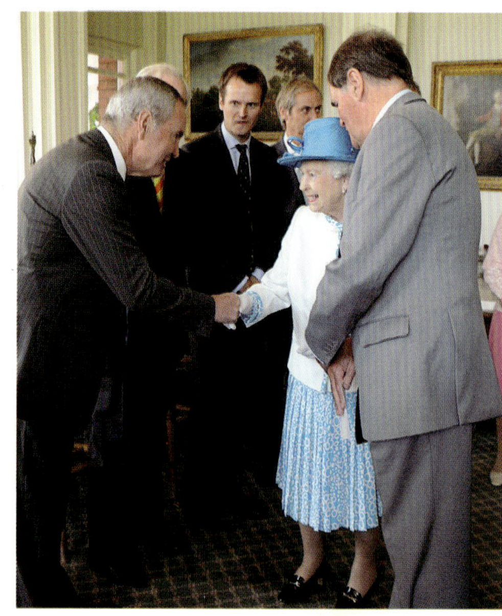

The Committee Room

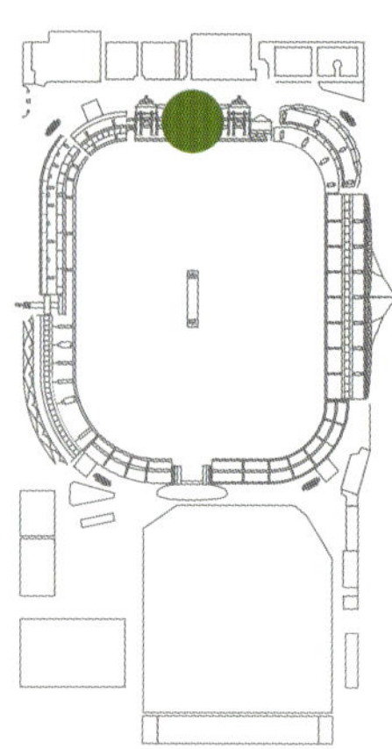

While all MCC and Middlesex Members may enjoy the Long Room on a match day, the Committee Room is reserved for the Committee and select guests. It is the meeting room of the Club and the scene of some of the most famous discussions and decisions in cricket's history. These include responses to the 'Bodyline' controversy (relating to England's bowling tactics in Australia in the 1932–3 Test Series), the D'Oliveira affair of 1968 (involving the controversial omission of a non-white player of South African origin from an England team to tour apartheid-era South Africa) and the rebel World Series Cricket tournament set up by Kerry Packer in 1977.

MCC published its first revised code of Laws in 1788, just one year after the Club was founded. It has retained guardianship of the Laws ever since, with the most recent revision published in 2017. This, the first complete new code of Laws to be issued since 2000, came into effect worldwide on 1 October 2017.

As an adjunct to its custodianship of the Laws and to provide a think-tank for those at the heart of the game, MCC established its World Cricket Committee in April 2006. An advisory body, it is comprised of current and former international cricketers and umpires from across the globe. The Committee's aims are as follows:

- to debate all matters in the interests of cricket and cricketers;
- to consider at all times the balance of the contest between bat and ball and to assist MCC's custodianship of the Laws of the Game;
- to protect the Spirit of Cricket; and
- to be sure that governing body decisions never put cash or country interests before the good of the game.

Above left: *A Portrait of the Mason Brothers, Harrow School* by Henry Walton, c.1770s.

Above right: Her Majesty The Queen meeting Members of the MCC Committee during the England v South Africa Test Match, 2017.

Right: A portrait of Lord Harris (1851–1932) by Arthur Hacker, RA, 1919. Lord Harris captained England in four Test Matches and later became a highly respected and influential administrator. He served as President of MCC in 1895, Trustee from 1906 to 1916 and Treasurer from 1916 until his death in 1932.

Below: The Committee Room set up for a meeting. The room has been the location for many momentous decisions in cricket's history, from changes to the Laws to the formation of ICC.

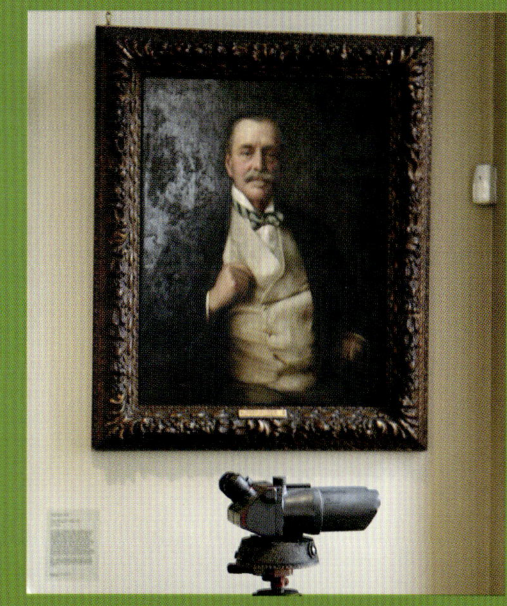

'There is no "secret chamber", for the Committee Room is simply divided from the centre room by two glass swing doors.'

From *Pavilions of Splendour*, ed. D. Hart-Davis (Methuen, 2004), p.27

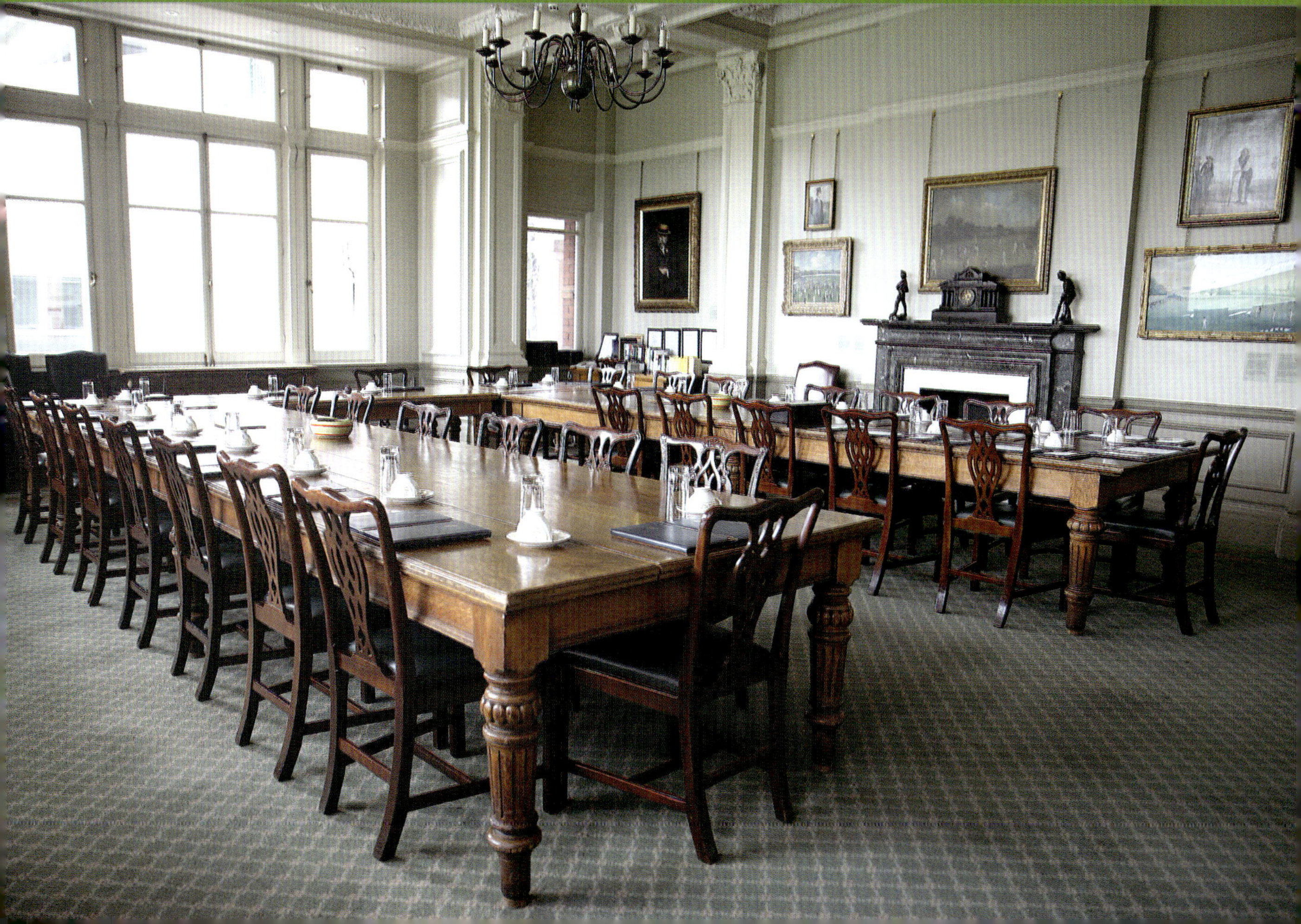

The Dressing Rooms

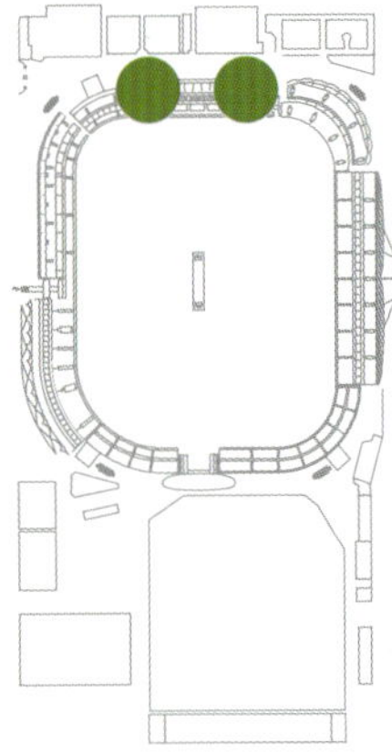

The first floor of the Pavilion houses the Dressing Rooms for players and Members, situated in the towers at either end of the building. The home side uses 'No. 1' in the south, the visitors 'No. 5' in the north. Both sets of players walk down one flight of the respective staircases, through the Long Room and out onto the pitch.

The Dressing Rooms are dominated by the famous Honours Boards that list the record feats of bowlers and batsmen in Tests at Lord's. The boards were first installed in 1992, with the Pakistan fast bowler Waqar Younis becoming the first to have his name added. The practice was quickly taken to heart by the players. It is now customary – indeed almost obligatory – for cricketers who have scored a century or taken five wickets to have their names taped up by their team-mates – even before the match has ended.

The first player to have his name taped up was South Africa's Jonty Rhodes in 1998. In doing so his team-mates unconsciously revived an old tradition begun by the Australian team in 1890. Its members inscribed their names on the terracotta tiles of the original balcony of the visitors' dressing room – now the Members' Bar.

Only one cricketer has the distinction of appearing on the Honours Boards in both dressing rooms. Gordon Greenidge made centuries for the West Indies against England in 1984 (214 not out) and 1988; he also made a century while representing MCC in the 1987 Bicentenary Match against a Rest of the World Eleven.

In 2019, as part of a refurbishment ahead of the ICC Men's World Cup, new Honours for Limited Overs International Cricket were introduced. This means recognition for some of the finest international innings played at the Ground, including centuries by Clive Lloyd and Sir Vivian Richards that won the first two World Cup Finals and, more recently, Anya Shrubsole's match-winning 6–46 against India in the 2017 ICC Women's World Cup Final.

Middlesex and county matches

The Home Dressing Room is also used by Middlesex for their county fixtures; since 1877 they have played the majority of their home matches at Lord's. Ever since their formation in 1864, Middlesex had struggled to find a permanent home. MCC had tried and failed to attract the county to play at Lord's in 1869 and 1874, but in 1876 – faced with the prospect of their favoured Prince's ground being redeveloped – Middlesex accepted a third offer. Their acceptance was despite some objections on the issue of finance and Lord's reputation as a bad ground for slow bowling.

In the late 19th century county cricket was growing in prestige, to the detriment of the Ground's regular programme of fixtures. It was essential for Lord's long-term survival that regular first-class cricket be played there, and just as essential to Middlesex's survival that they had a permanent home. Over 140 years later the original reasons for this long partnership remain as valid.

A typically cluttered scene in one of the Dressing Rooms on a match day.

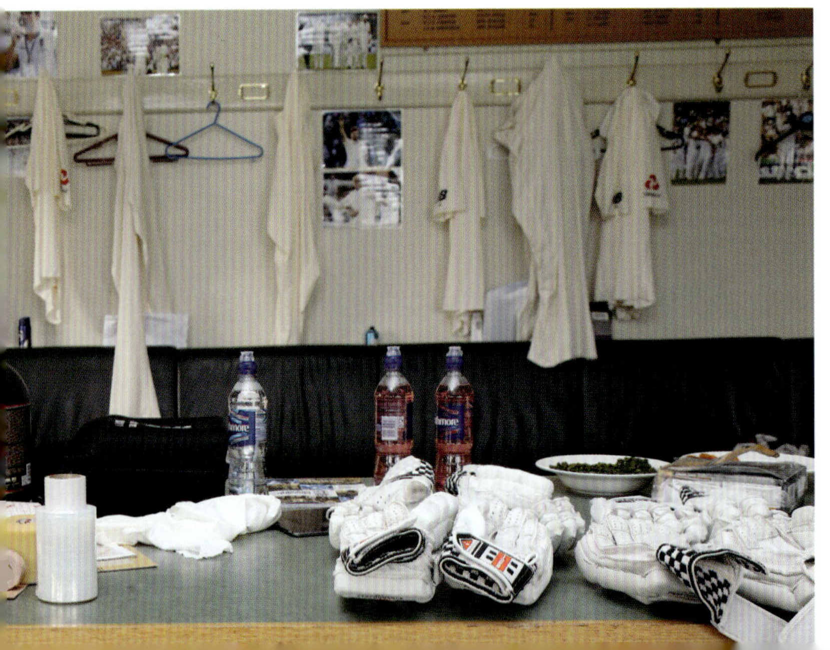

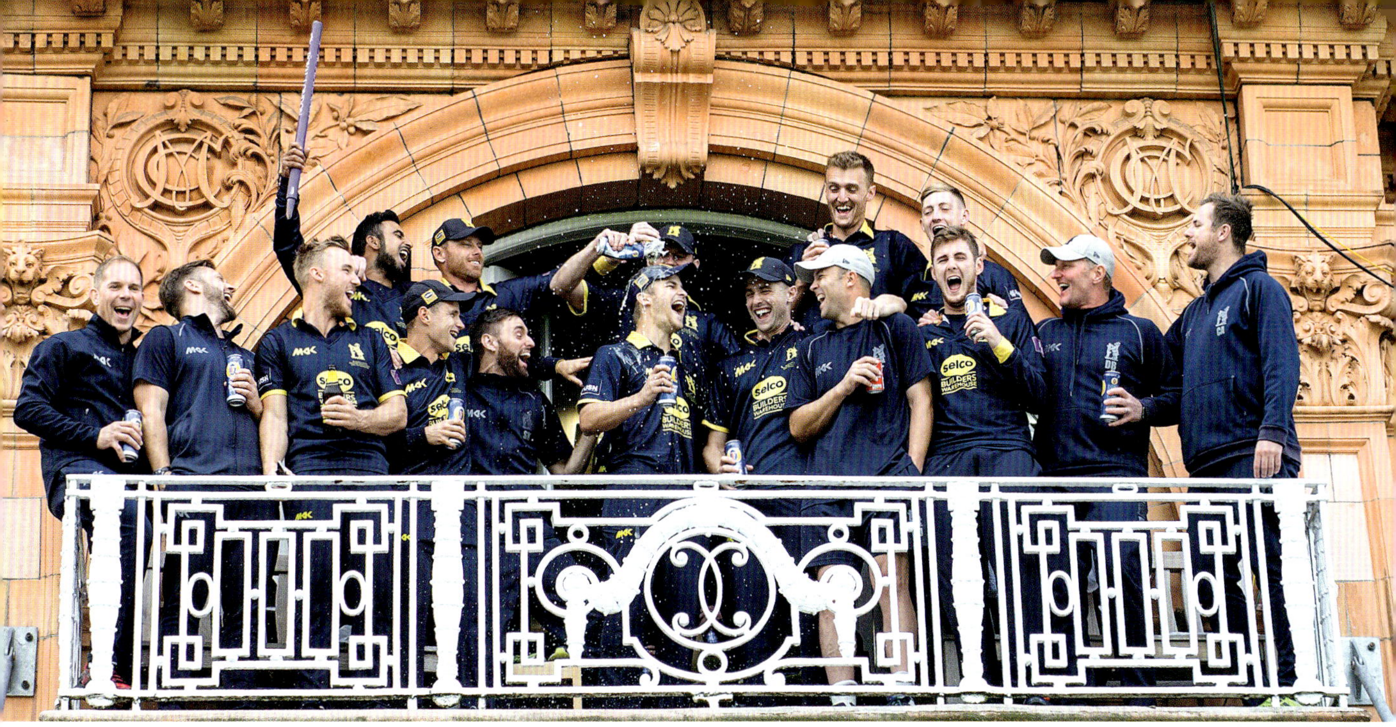

Top ten Test Match performances – batting

333	G.A. Gooch	England v India	1990
259	G.C. Smith	South Africa v England	2003
254	D.G. Bradman	Australia v England	1930
240	W.R. Hammond	England v Australia	1938
226	I.J.L. Trott	England v Bangladesh	2010
221	R.W.T. Key	England v West Indies	2004
215	S.P.D. Smith	Australia v England	2015
214*	C.G. Greenidge	West Indies v England	1984
211	J.B. Hobbs	England v South Africa	1924
208	D.C.S. Compton	England v South Africa	1947

Highest scores for other countries

206	M.P. Donnelly	New Zealand v England	1949
202	Mohammad Yousuf	Pakistan v England	2006
193	T.M. Dilshan	Sri Lanka v England	2011
184	M.H. Mankad	India v England	1952
103	Tamim Iqbal	Bangladesh v England	2010
68	D.D. Ebrahim	Zimbabwe v England	2003

Top ten Test Match performances – bowling

8–34	I.T. Botham	England v Pakistan	1978
8–38	G.D. McGrath	Australia v England	1997
8–43	H. Verity	England v Australia	1934
8–51	D.L. Underwood	England v Pakistan	1974
8–53	R.A.L. Massie	Australia v England	1972
8–84	R.A.L. Massie	Australia v England	1972
8–103	I.T. Botham	England v West Indies	1984
7–32	D.L. Underwood	England v New Zealand	1969
7–36	G. Ulyett	England v Australia	1884
7–39	J.B. Statham	England v South Africa	1955

Best bowling for other countries

7–65	S.J. Pegler	South Africa v England	1912
7–74	I. Sharma	India v England	2014
6–32	Mudassar Nazar	Pakistan v England	1982
6–32	M.D. Marshall	West Indies v England	1988
6–50	T.G. Southee	New Zealand v England	2013
6–87	H.H. Streak	Zimbabwe v England	2000
5–69	R.J. Ratnayake	Sri Lanka v England	1991
5–98	Shahadat Hossain	Bangladesh v England	2010

Above: Warwickshire players celebrate their victory over Surrey in the 2016 Royal London One Day Final.

Below: Sri Lanka's Kumar Sangakkara points to his his name on the visitors' Honours Board after his century in his fourth Test at Lord's in 2014.

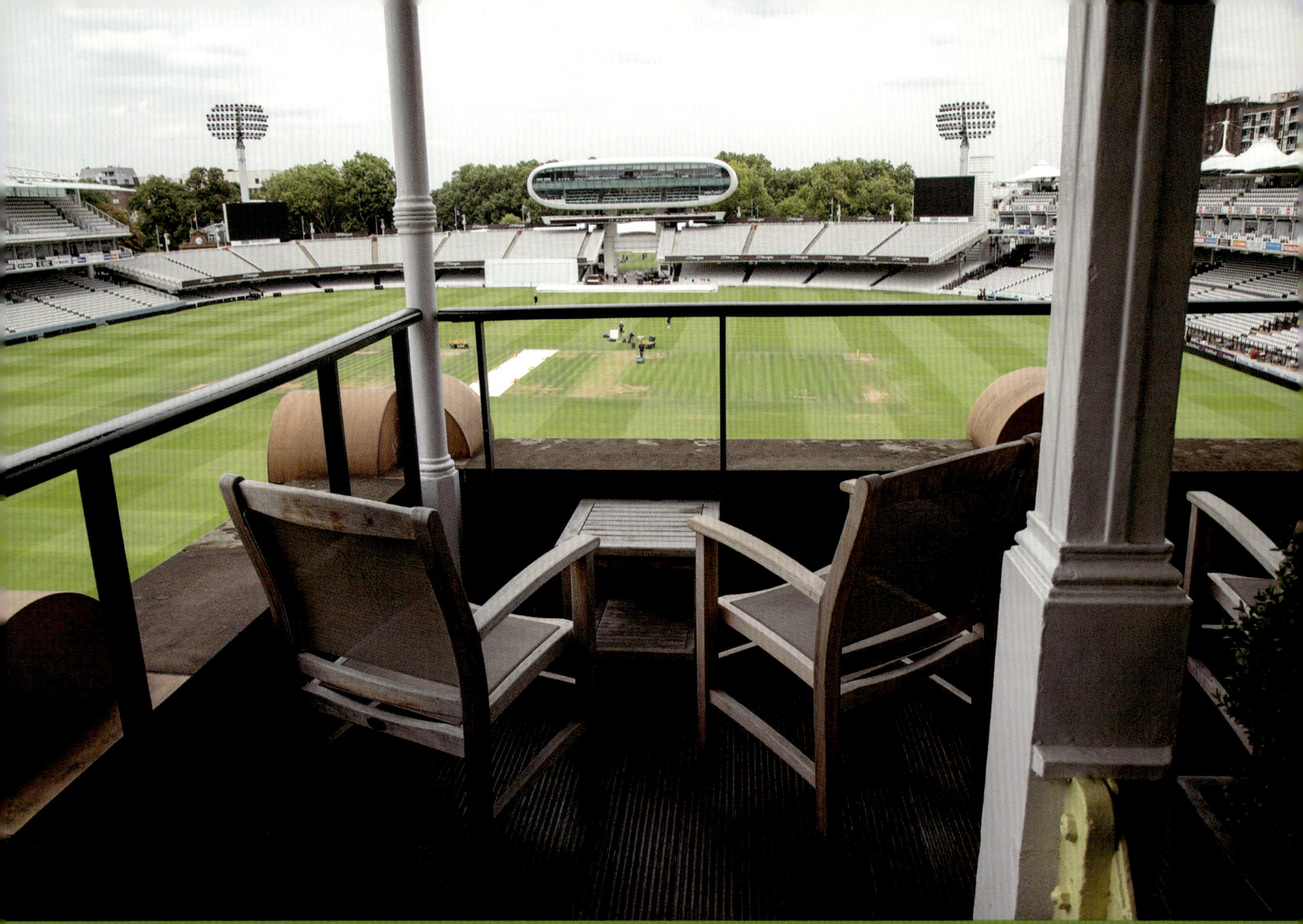

Above: The view from the Pavilion Roof Terrace, looking east towards the Media Centre and Nursery Ground, is one of the finest at Lord's.

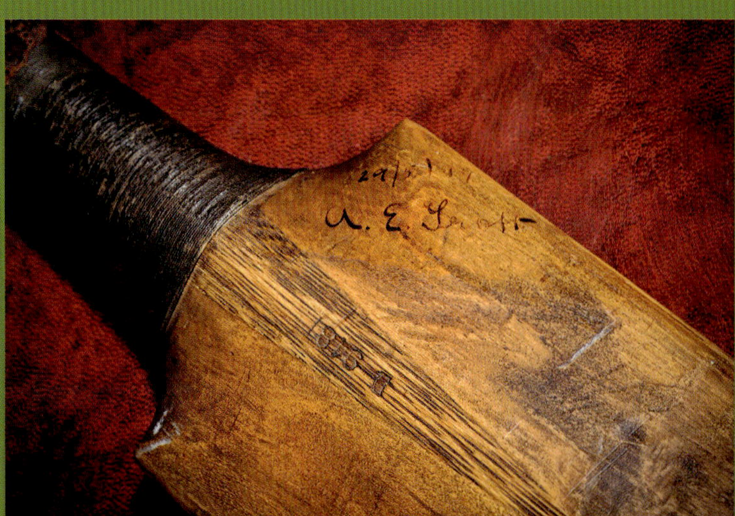

Right: Albert Trott's signature on the back of the bat he used to strike the ball over the Pavilion roof in 1899. Having played three Tests for his native Australia, Albert Trott remade his career in England after his controversial omission from the Australian touring side in 1896, a team captained by his own brother Harry. Qualifying for Middlesex after two years' residence, Trott went on to play Test cricket for England as well.

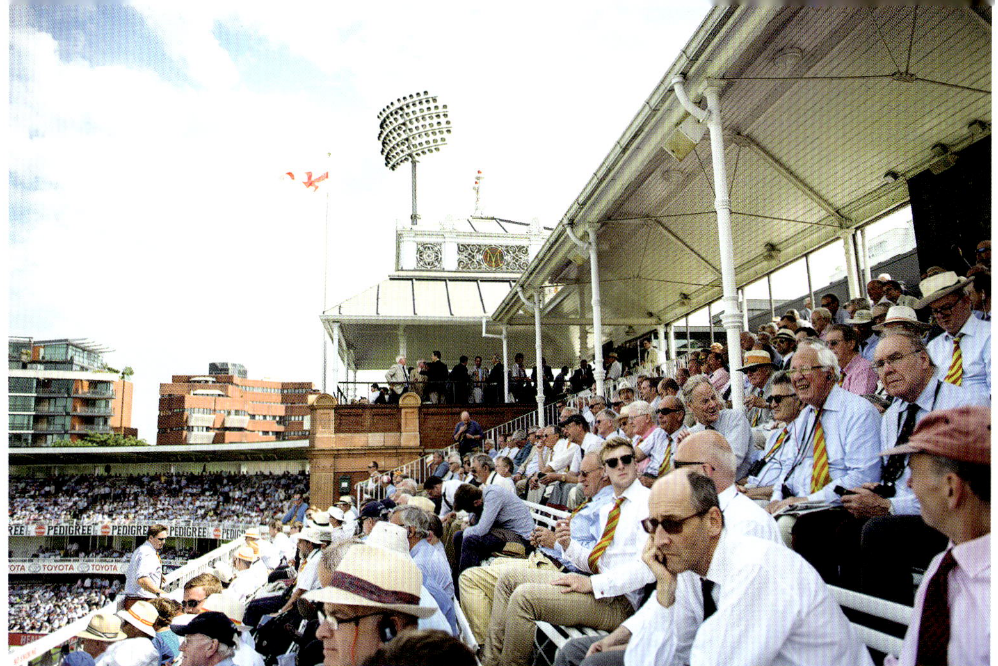

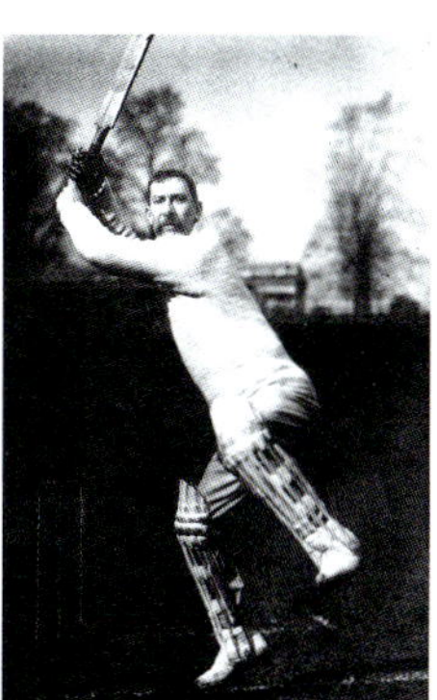

Left: MCC Members follow the action from the upper balcony of the Pavilion during the 2017 England v South Africa Test Match.

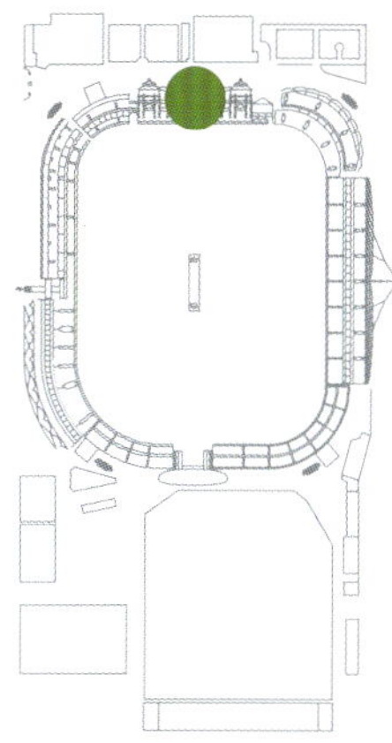

Below: Albert Trott jumps out to drive in a photograph by George Beldam, *c.*1904.

The Roof Terrace

The Pavilion Roof Terrace was only finally laid out in 2005, following a refurbishment programme that restored the building to its full Victorian splendour. From 1973 to 1999 the north turret had contained the broadcast commentary box from which BBC radio's *Test Match Special* was delivered.

It now offers arguably the best views at Lord's, providing an ideal stage to appreciate one of the most remarkable cricketing feats ever to take place here. On 31 July 1899 Middlesex's Australian all-rounder Albert Trott, playing against the country of his birth, struck a ball from Monty Noble straight over the Pavilion roof. The ball glanced off one of the tall chimney stacks before landing in the garden of the Dressing Room attendant's house, where the Museum and Real Tennis court now stand. Huge as Trott's hit was, it did not entirely leave the ground, and so the batsman was awarded only four runs, according to the Laws of Cricket at the time.

He remains the only man to have achieved the feat of hitting the ball over the Pavilion, however, although a few others have come close. Glamorgan's Mike Llewellyn struck one of the turrets in the 1977 Gillette Cup Final, while Australia's Kim Hughes struck Chris Old into the top tier during the 1980 Centenary Test Match. In 2010 Somerset's Kieron Pollard almost matched Trott during a Twenty20 game when his massive strike cleared the roof – only to bounce off the wall at the back of the Terrace.

'Trott began with a "sighter" on to the first balcony, and then came this stupendous straight drive, the ball landing in the garden of one of the houses.'

Pelham Warner, *Lord's 1787–1945* (George Harrap, 1946), p.121

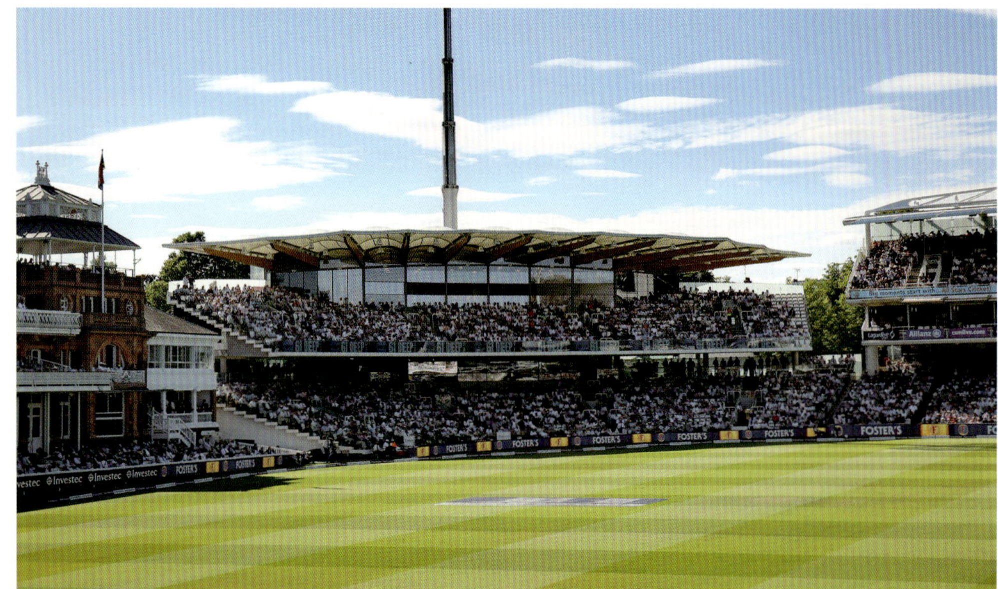

The new Warner Stand, completed in 2017, filled with spectators on a Test Match day. Its height has been carefully calculated to sit well with the collection of buildings at Lord's, particularly the Grade II* listed Pavilion.

The Warner Stand

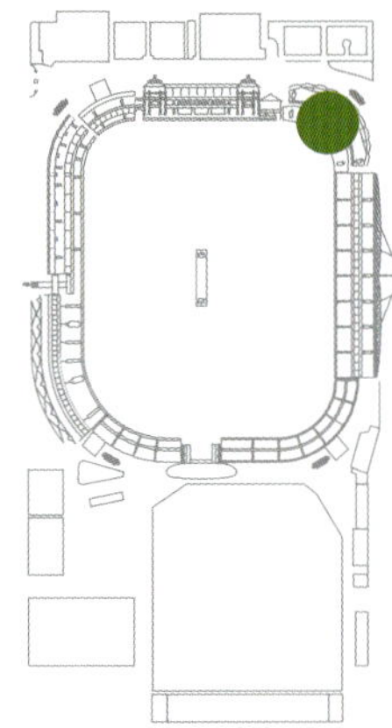

Until 1958 all spectator stands at Lord's were identified by a letter of the alphabet, running clockwise around the Ground. What is now known as the Warner Stand was 'A' enclosure and amounted to no more than a few rows of covered seating. This was because the 'coach mound' – a raised area of grass lined with trees – stood behind it; tradition dictated that for some of the oldest fixtures visitors could watch the match from horse-drawn carriages parked there.

The 1950s stand was itself replaced in 2015–17, and the current construction continues an innovative tradition of architecture at Lord's. It sports a canopy of translucent tensile fabric supported on American White Oak beams, ensuring that spectators benefit from both shade and natural light. The canopy is the first use of this kind of fabric in Europe.

Both stands honoured a man whose connection with Lord's spanned almost 70 years and is almost unparalleled in its significance and wide-ranging contribution to cricket. Sir Pelham 'Plum' Warner was a player for both Middlesex and England. He was also an influential administrator (President of MCC), Test Selector and Tour Manager on the infamous 'Bodyline' tour to Australia in 1932–3. Warner also made a noted literary contribution to the game. He was the author of *How We Recovered the Ashes*, the book that cemented cricket's association with the Ashes, and editor of the famous *Cricketer* magazine from 1921 to 1962.

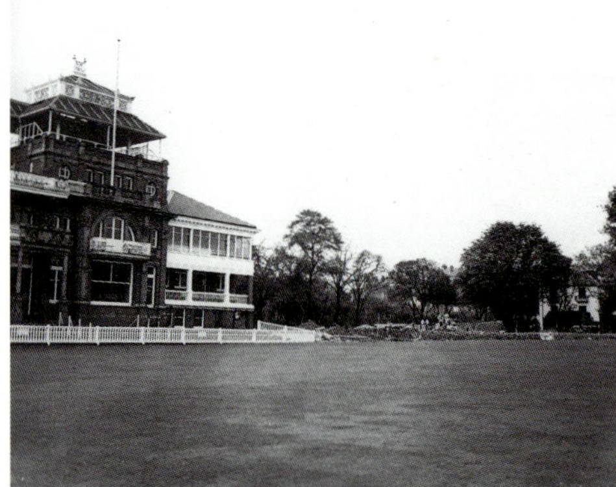

Demolition of the old 'A' enclosure in 1957 prior to the construction of the original Warner Stand, designed by Kenneth Peacock, the following year.

Right: Pelham Warner and his MCC team for the Club's first full overseas tour to Australia in 1903–4.

Below: The magnificent roof canopy of the new Warner Stand is the latest example of innovative architectural design at Lord's. The canopy is formed from translucent tensile fabric – the first use of this kind of fabric in Europe. Sustainability is also important, with solar thermal and photovoltaic roof panels incorporated to generate hot water and electricity.

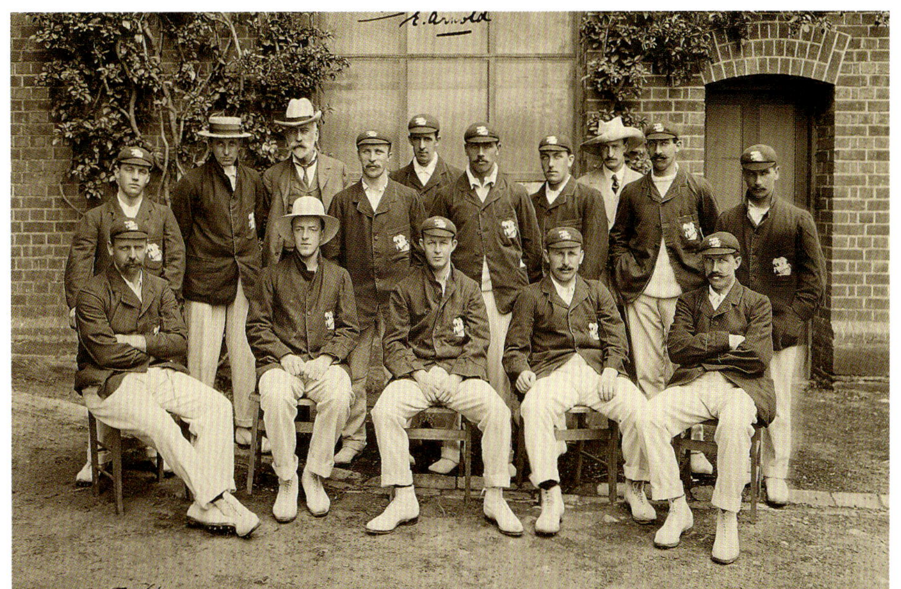

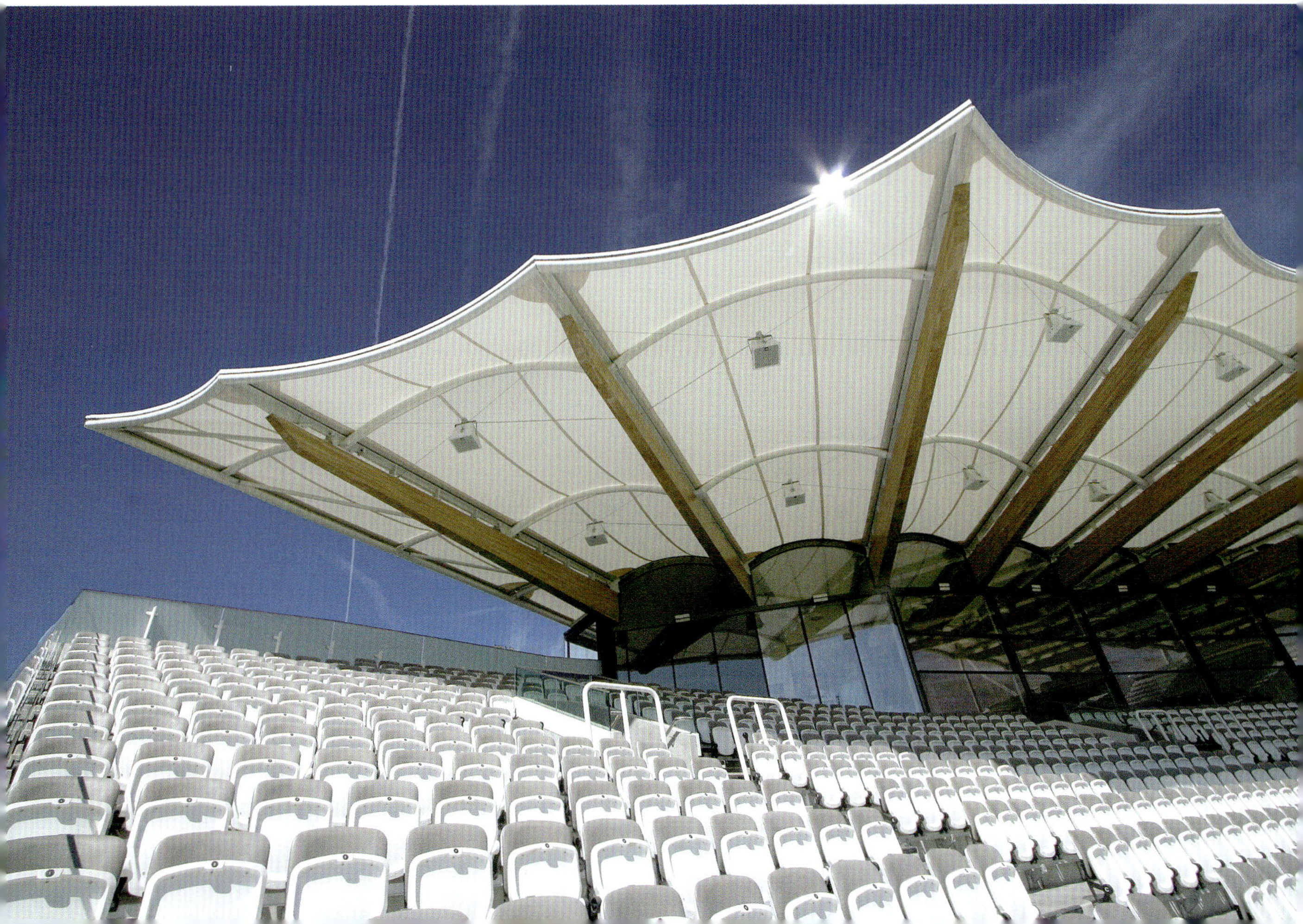

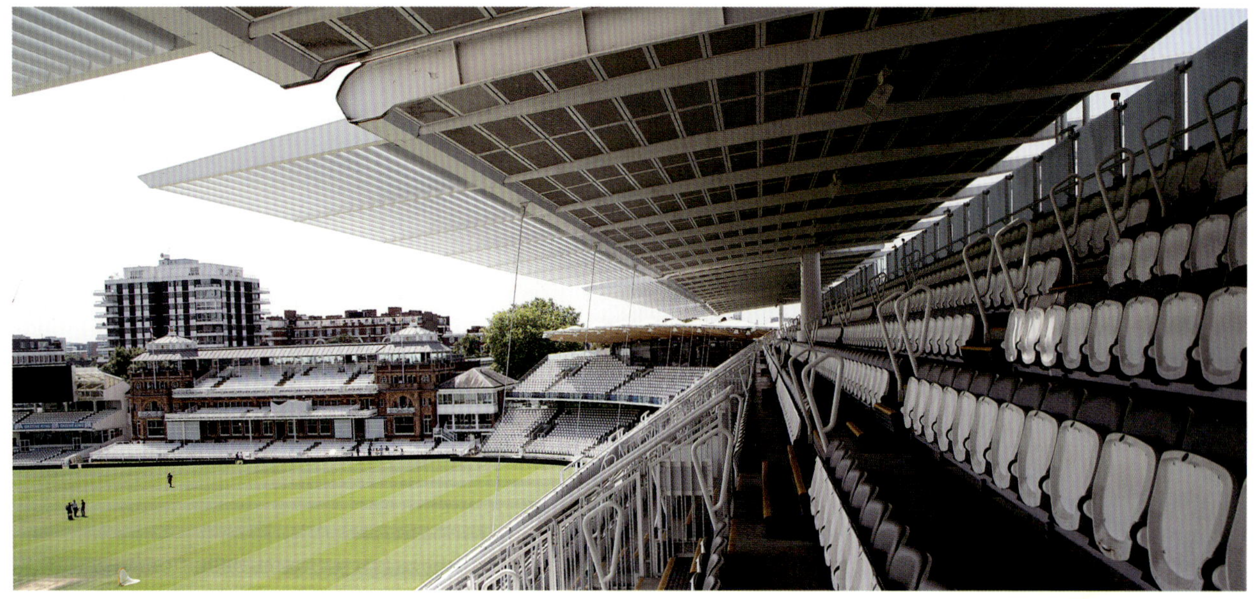

The Grand Stand

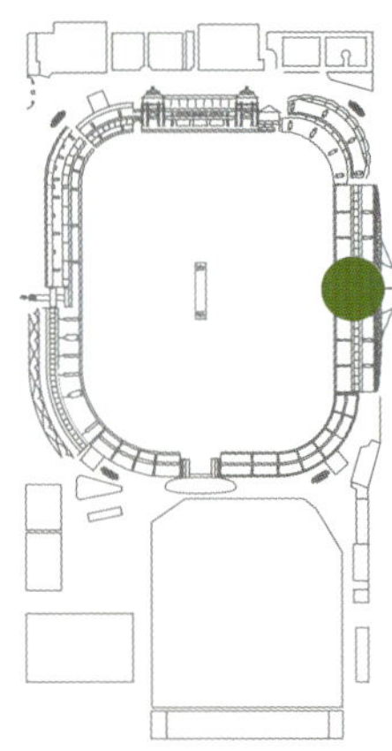

The first Grand Stand to be constructed on this site was opened in 1867. It included the first dedicated accommodation for the press at Lord's. The stand was funded by a private consortium led by MCC's then Secretary R.A. Fitzgerald; it proved so profitable that after two years the Club opted to purchase it back. The Stand underwent many alterations and extensions during its life before it was finally demolished at the end of the 1925 season.

MCC chose Sir Herbert Baker as the architect to design its replacement. He had already worked at Lord's as designer of the Grace Gates (p.6) and would continue to be involved with MCC until his death in 1946. Baker made his name as a young architect in South Africa, and also worked with the renowned Edwin Lutyens in New Delhi. His new Grand Stand opened in time for the England v Australia Test Match in June 1926. It was a visually striking building, with the now famous Father Time weather vane perched above the central scoreboard (p.42).

The current Grand Stand, designed by Nicholas Grimshaw, was completed in 1998. It is constructed entirely of pre-fabricated sections and has a lower terrace around 100 metres in length; the superstructure is supported on just three concrete columns. Today's Grand Stand holds 6,200 spectators and has twenty hospitality boxes.

Above: The Grand Stand during preparations for the 2018 England v India Test Match.

Right: Father Time stands above the scoreboard on Sir Herbert Baker's Grand Stand, in a photograph from the 1966 England v West Indies Test Match.

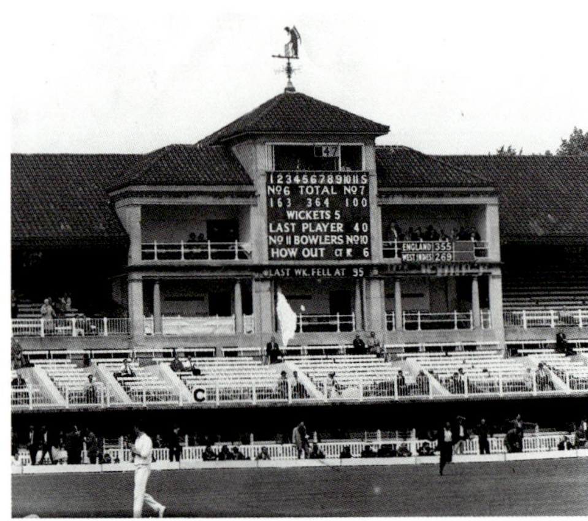

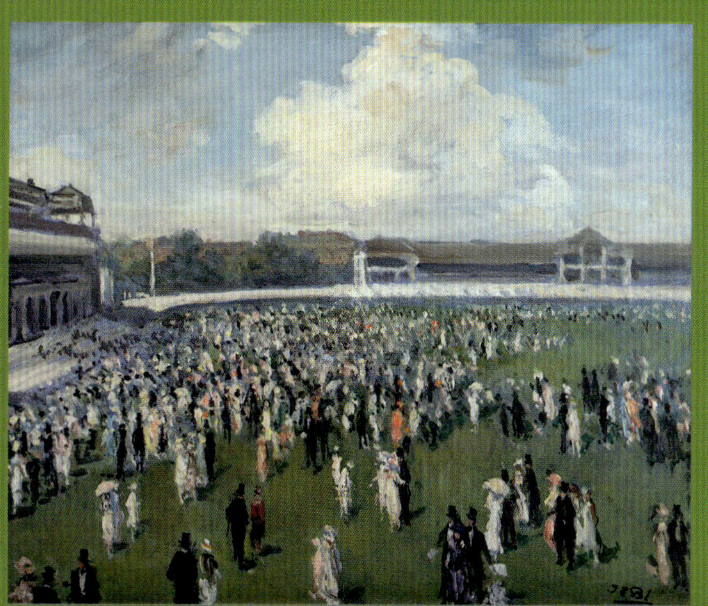

'It is greatly in its favour that it has dignity, and blends in well with the Pavilion.'

E.W. Swanton, *Follow On* (Collins, 1977)

Left: *L'Heure du Thé* by Jacques-Emile Blanche (c.1928) shows perambulation during an Eton v Harrow match. Sir Herbert Baker's Grand Stand appears in the background. The Eton v Harrow match, first played at Lord's in 1805, remains an annual fixture.

Below: A dramatic sunset behind the Grand Stand during a Middlesex v Essex Twenty20 match in 2017. Middlesex won by 72 runs.

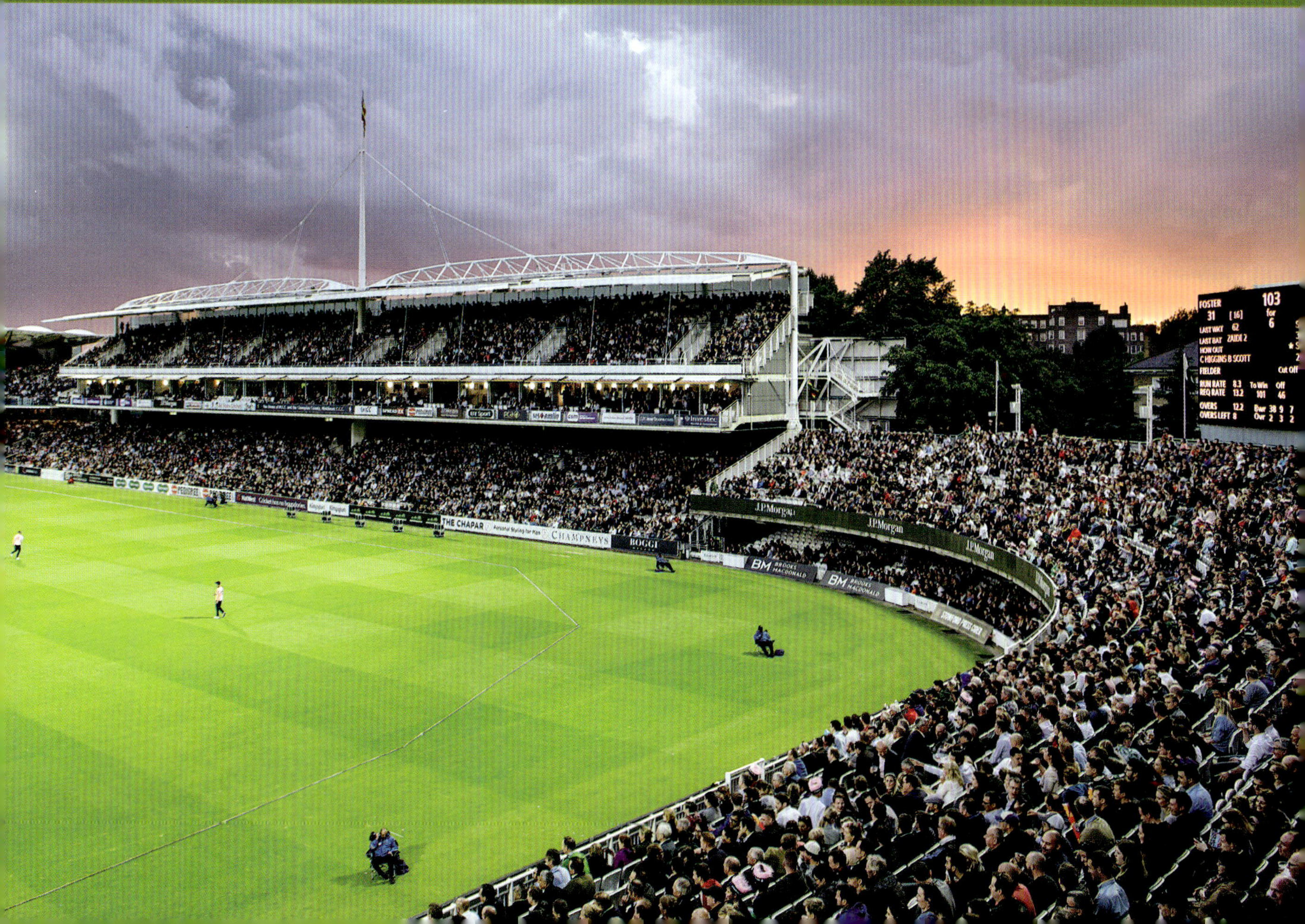

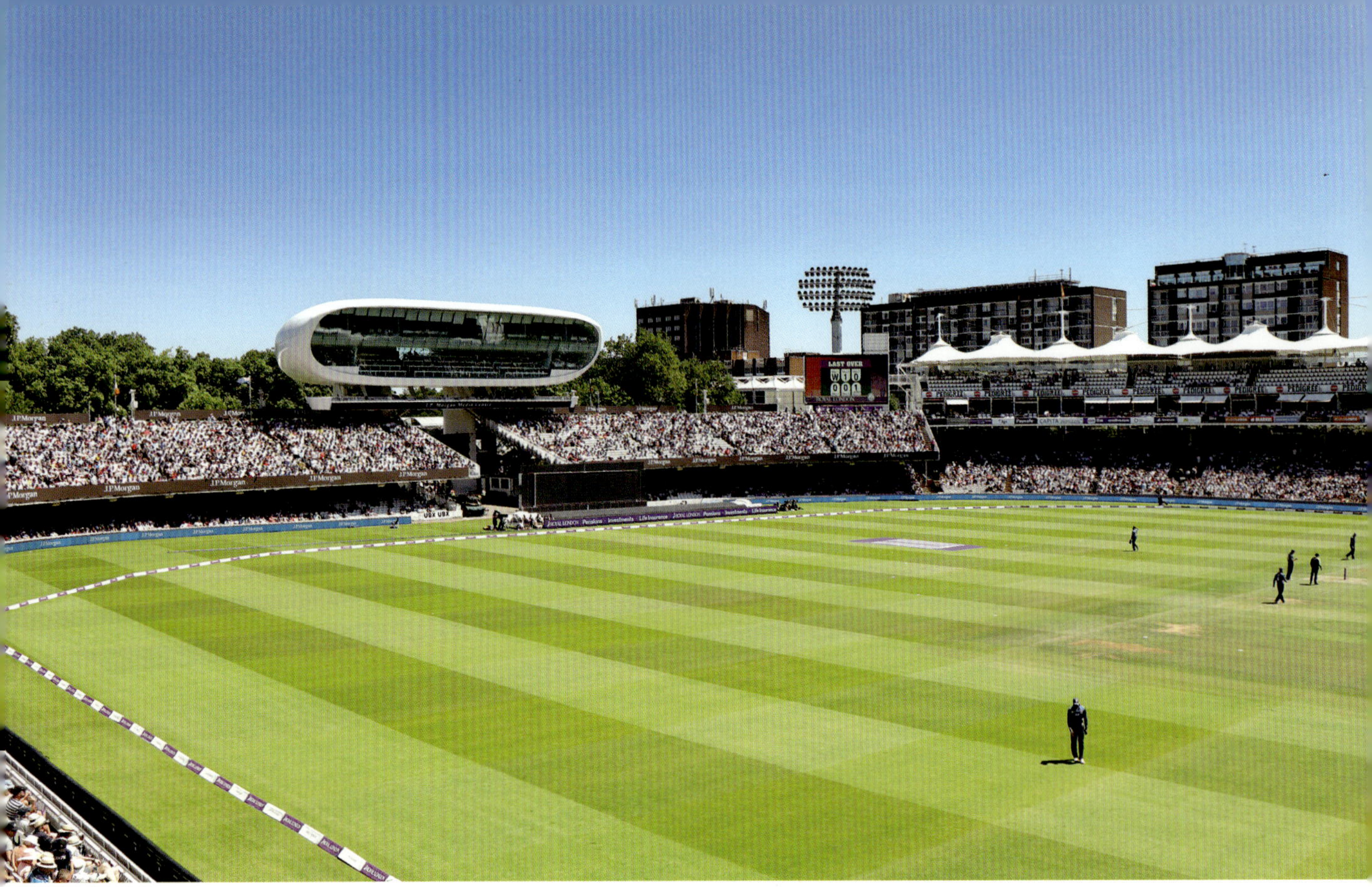

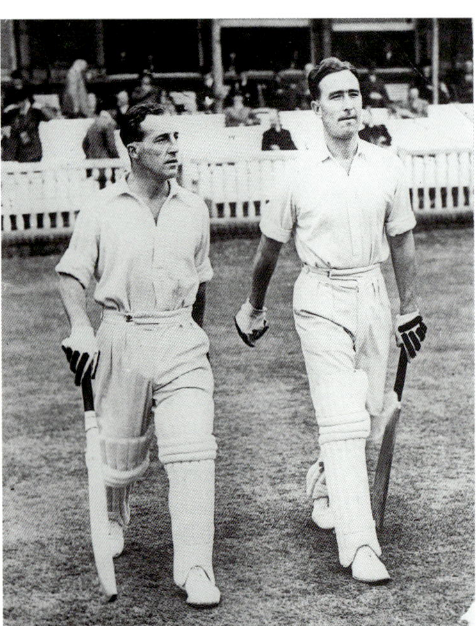

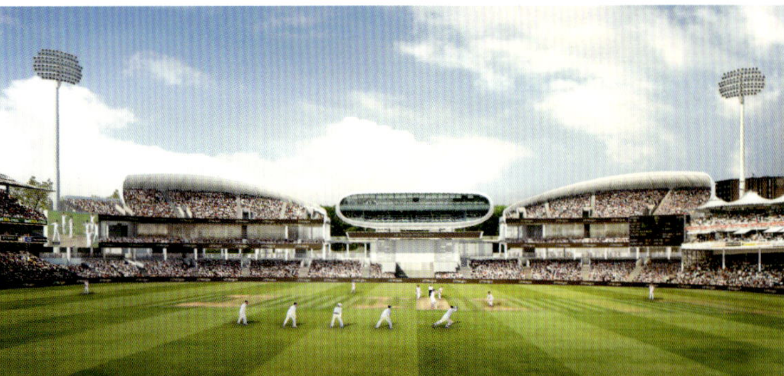

Left: Bill Edrich (left) and Denis Compton (right) walk out to bat at Lord's during the golden summer of 1947. In glorious weather, the pair's magnificent run-scoring helped the public to forget the hardships of war, rationing and economic austerity.

Top: Spectators pack out the Compton and Edrich Stands during a sunny Royal London One Day Final between Hampshire and Kent in 2018.

Above: Designs for the proposed new Compton and Edrich Stands by WilkinsonEyre.

John Arlott, *Vintage Summer: 1947*
(Eyre & Spottiswoode, 1967)

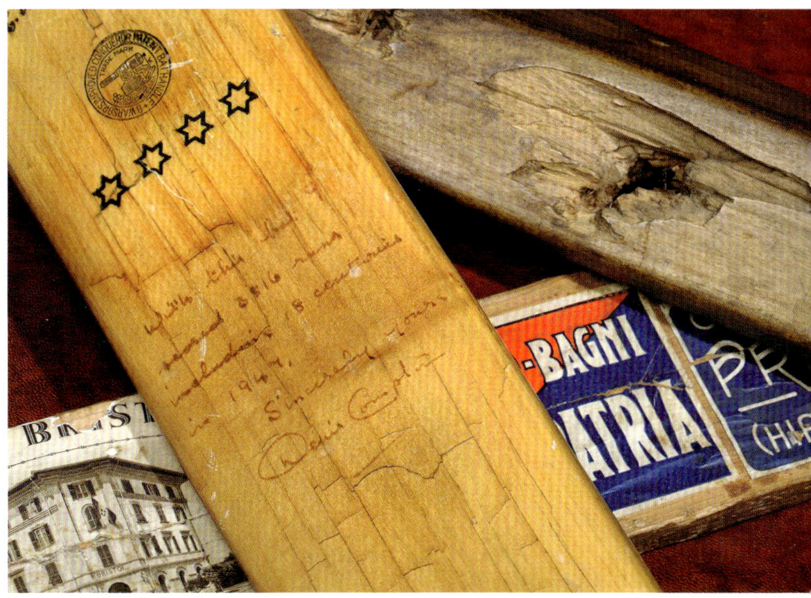

The Compton and Edrich Stands

The next phase in the redevelopment of Lord's is the rebuilding of the Compton and Edrich Stands, scheduled for completion in 2021. The new three-tier stands will accommodate around 11,500 spectators; unlike the existing structures, the new stands' top tier will be partially covered. The designs are the work of two-time Stirling Prize winners WilkinsonEyre, the architects responsible for the refurbishment of the Grade II*-listed Battersea Power Station.

Following the tradition established by the Warner and Allen Stands, MCC made an obvious and appropriate selection of a Middlesex and England pairing for these twin structures.

Denis Compton first came to prominence as a dashing, sometimes unorthodox batsman in the 1930s. However, it was his performances in the golden summer of 1947, in which he scored 3,816 first-class runs including eighteen centuries (nine of them at Lord's), that raised him to greatness. He toured Australia for the 1950–1 Ashes Series, serving as Vice-Captain, and became the first professional to captain MCC for an entire game. In 1953 Compton

struck the winning runs that reclaimed the Ashes for England after twenty years. He was also an accomplished footballer who played most of his career at Arsenal.

Bill Edrich made an immediate impression as an attacking young Middlesex batsman in the mid-1930s, but his early scores for England were meagre. However, he made 219 in the famous ten-day 'timeless' Test against South Africa in 1938–9 and never looked back. Edrich shared Denis Compton's glory in the summer of 1947, scoring 3,539 first-class runs – including twelve centuries.

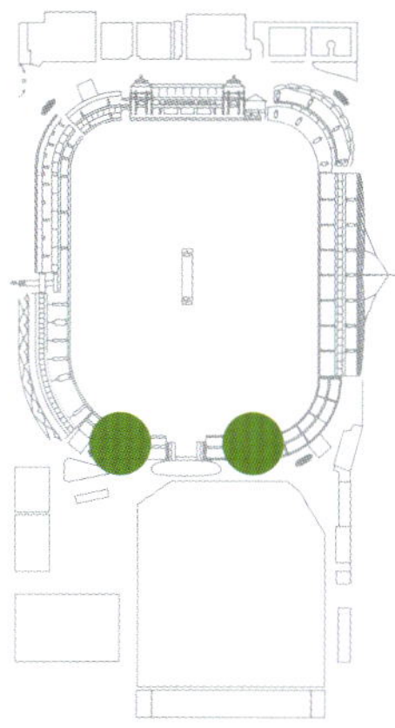

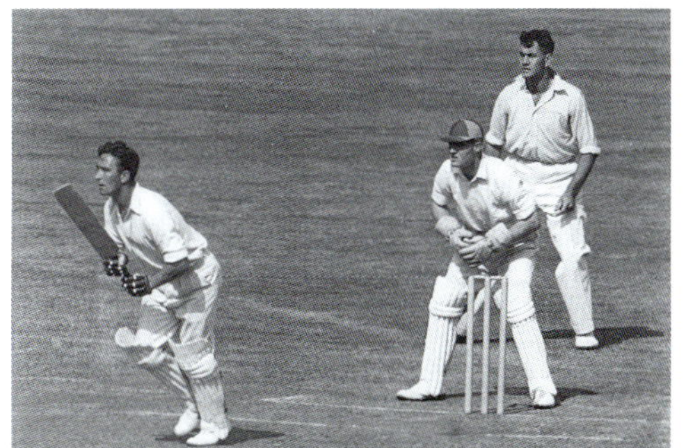

Above: The bat used by Denis Compton during the 1947 season, together with other items from the MCC Collections.

Left: Denis Compton batting for Middlesex against Surrey in 1948. Compton made 123* in just two and a quarter hours as Middlesex romped to victory by an innings and four runs.

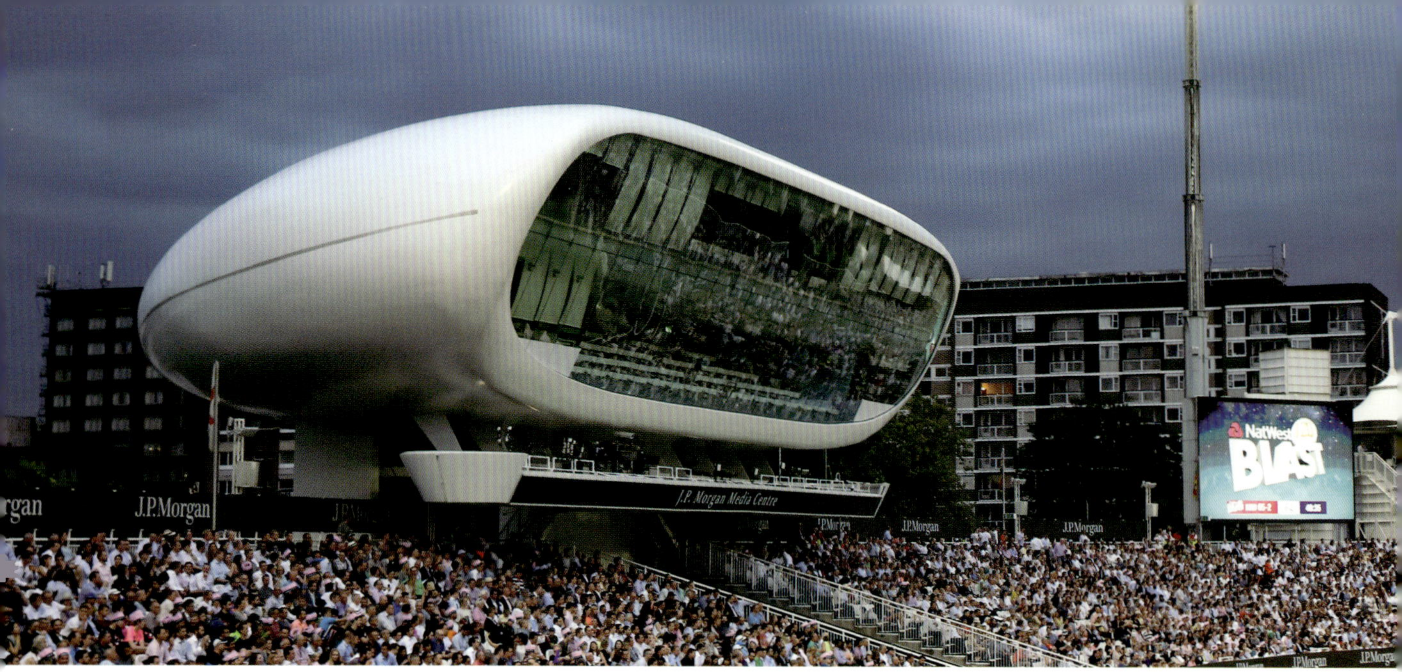

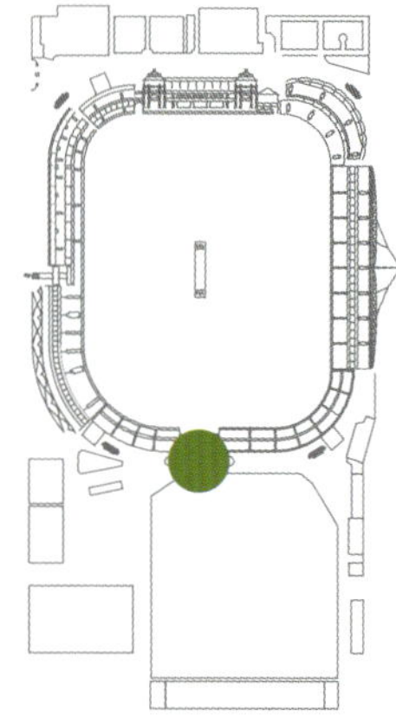

The J.P. Morgan Media Centre

In 1999 the Lord's skyline acquired a dramatic addition in the shape of the new Media Centre. With the Ground scheduled to host the ICC World Cup Final, it was clear that the existing media facilities, concentrated in the Warner Stand and the north turret of the Pavilion, were far from adequate to accommodate the more than 200 journalists, photographers and broadcasters expected to attend.

The Nursery End offered the only possible prospect of a view from behind the bowler's arm without disturbing the Grade II* listed Pavilion. The site came with challenges, however; the gap between the Compton and Edrich Stands was very small and access to the playing area for ground staff was still required. Clearly the new design would have to 'float' above the existing buildings.

The concept, created by Future Systems architects, involved a 'pod', constructed at the Pendennis shipyard in Cornwall and designed to rest on two reinforced concrete supports. The final Centre was widely acclaimed and won several awards, including the prestigious Stirling Prize for Architecture in 1999.

Twenty years on, Lord's prepared to host its fifth Men's World Cup Final in 2019. The J.P. Morgan Media Centre was closed over two winter periods for refurbishment, to enable an even greater number of press to attend.

Above: A close-up view of the J.P. Morgan Media Centre. Prior to its construction most of the media were housed in the old Warner Stand, while the Test Match Special broadcasting box was in the north turret of the Pavilion.

Right: MCC Chief Executive Guy Lavender in conversation with Jonathan Agnew in the Test Match Special box during the England v India Test Match in 2018.

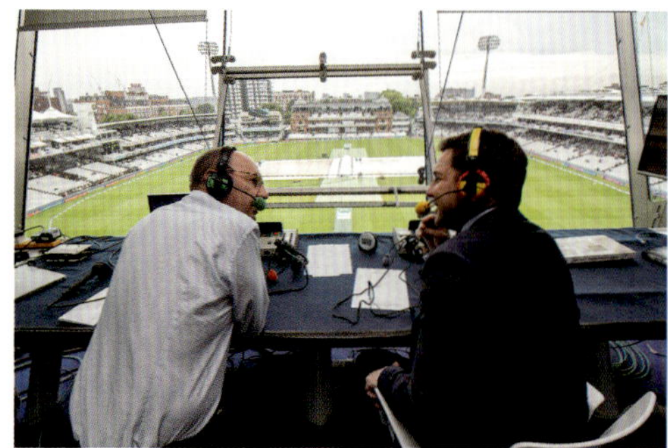

Right: Cleaning the window
of the Test Match Special
commentary box, 2017.

Below: Cricket writers
and journalists fill the J.P.
Morgan Media Centre
during the 2018 England v
India Test Match. On any
match day there is space
for more than 100 print and
online journalists, together
with broadcasting studios
for television and radio
and a working area for
photographers.

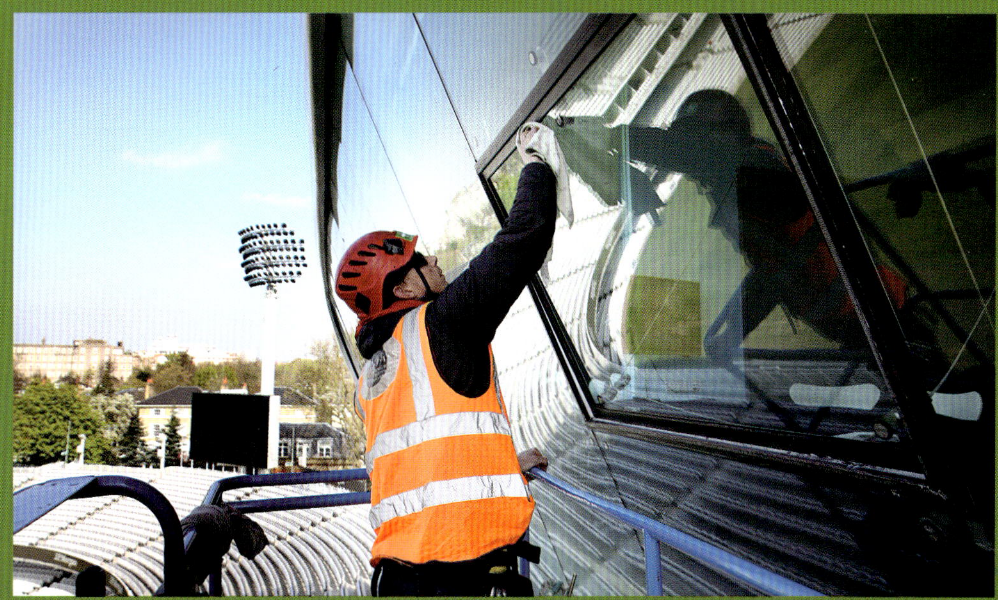

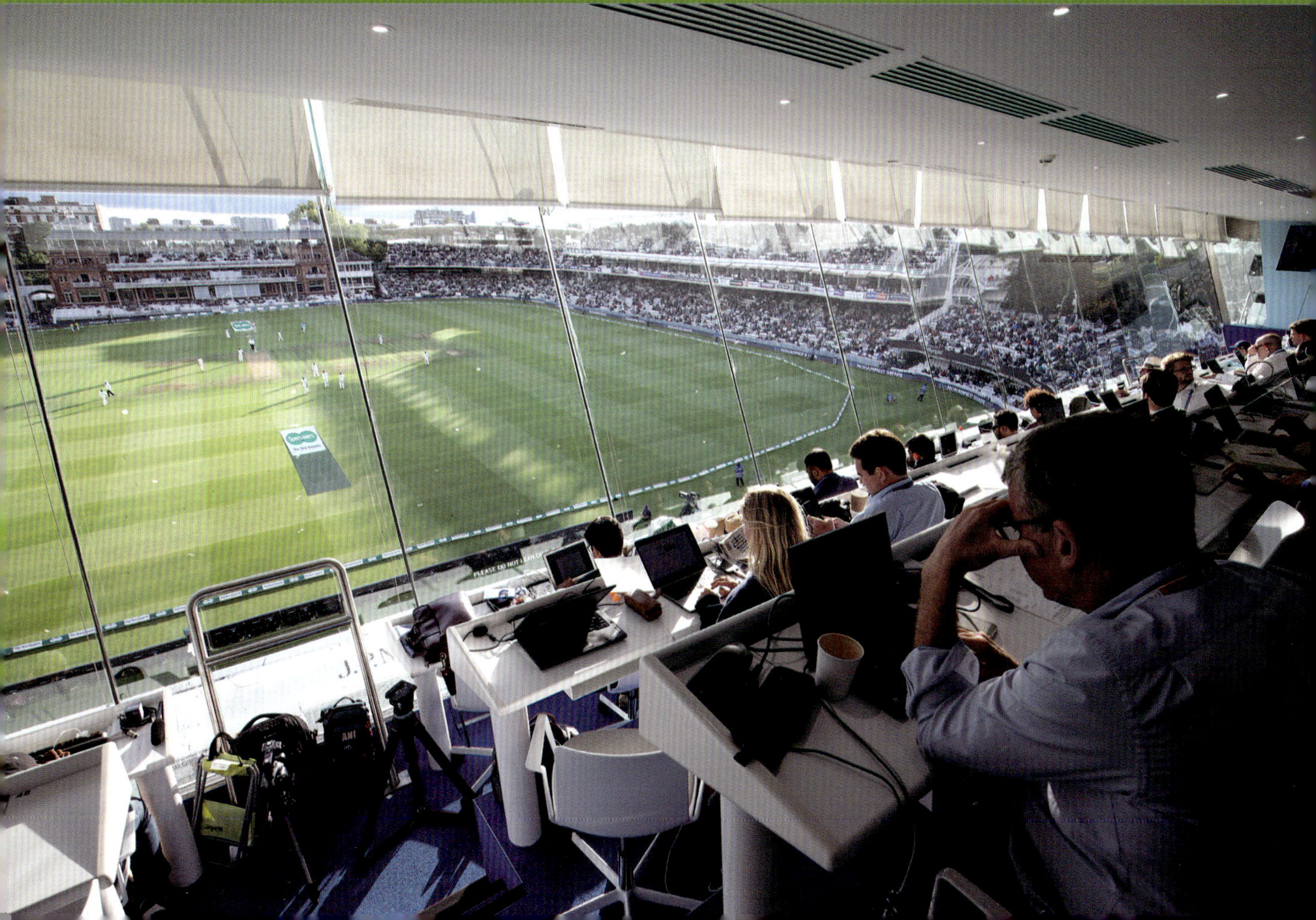

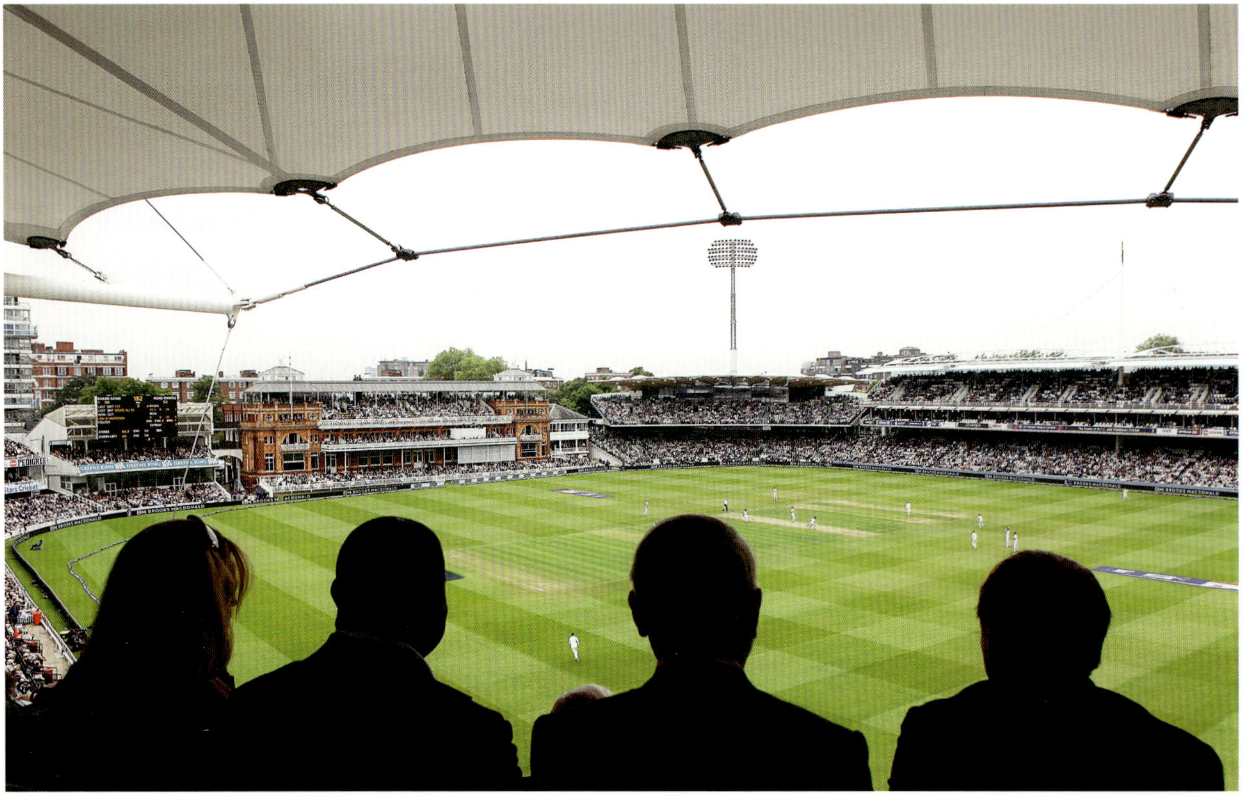

Above: View from the top of the Mound Stand during the 2018 England v Pakistan Test Match.

Right: The brickwork colonnade of the original Mound Stand, designed by Frank Verity in 1898, remains an integral part of its modern successor.

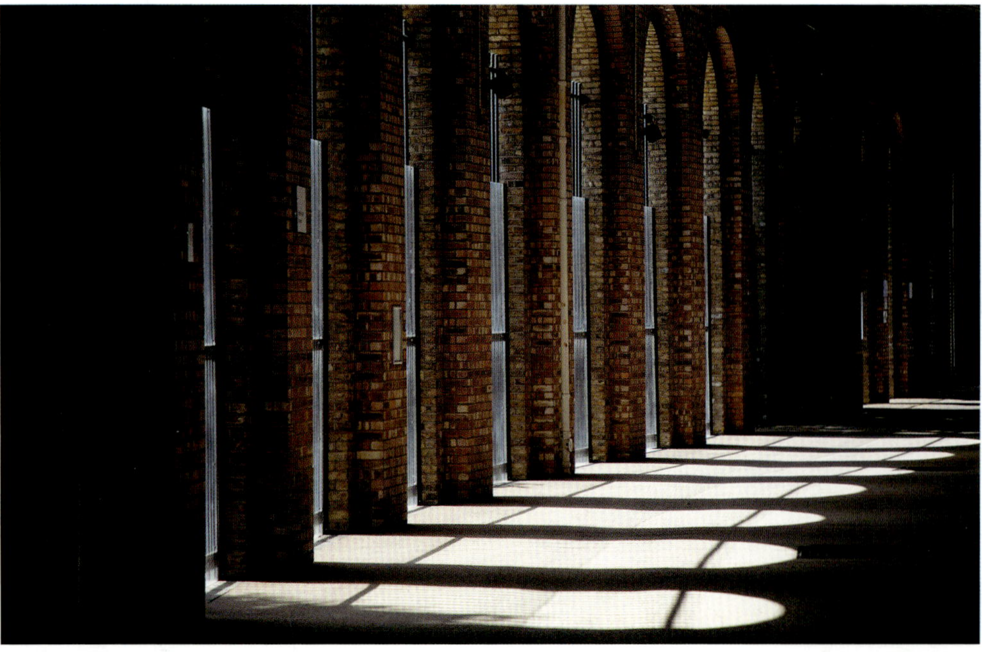

The Mound Stand

On the east side of the Ground is the Mound Stand, rebuilt and opened in 1987 to commemorate the bicentenary of MCC. Greatly facilitated by a most generous gift from Sir Paul Getty, KBE, the stand was designed by Sir Michael Hopkins and has received many accolades from the architectural world. Its roof structure, inspired by the Pavilion, has a PVC-coated canopy resembling the tents and marquees of village cricket; it has since been replicated in cricket grounds all over the world.

The original terrace of the old Mound Stand, designed by Frank Verity in 1898, was incorporated into Hopkins' design. The stylish colonnade of brick arches can be seen to best effect from the rear. The terrace remains a firm favourite as a place to watch the cricket, particularly when bathed in late afternoon sunshine.

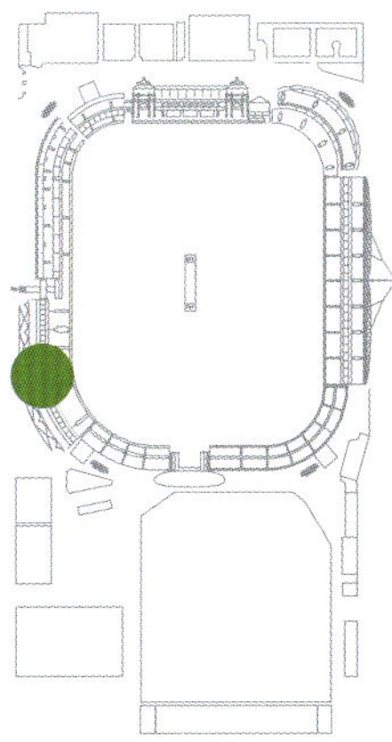

The Mound Stand under floodlights during a Twenty20 game between Middlesex and Surrey in 2016.

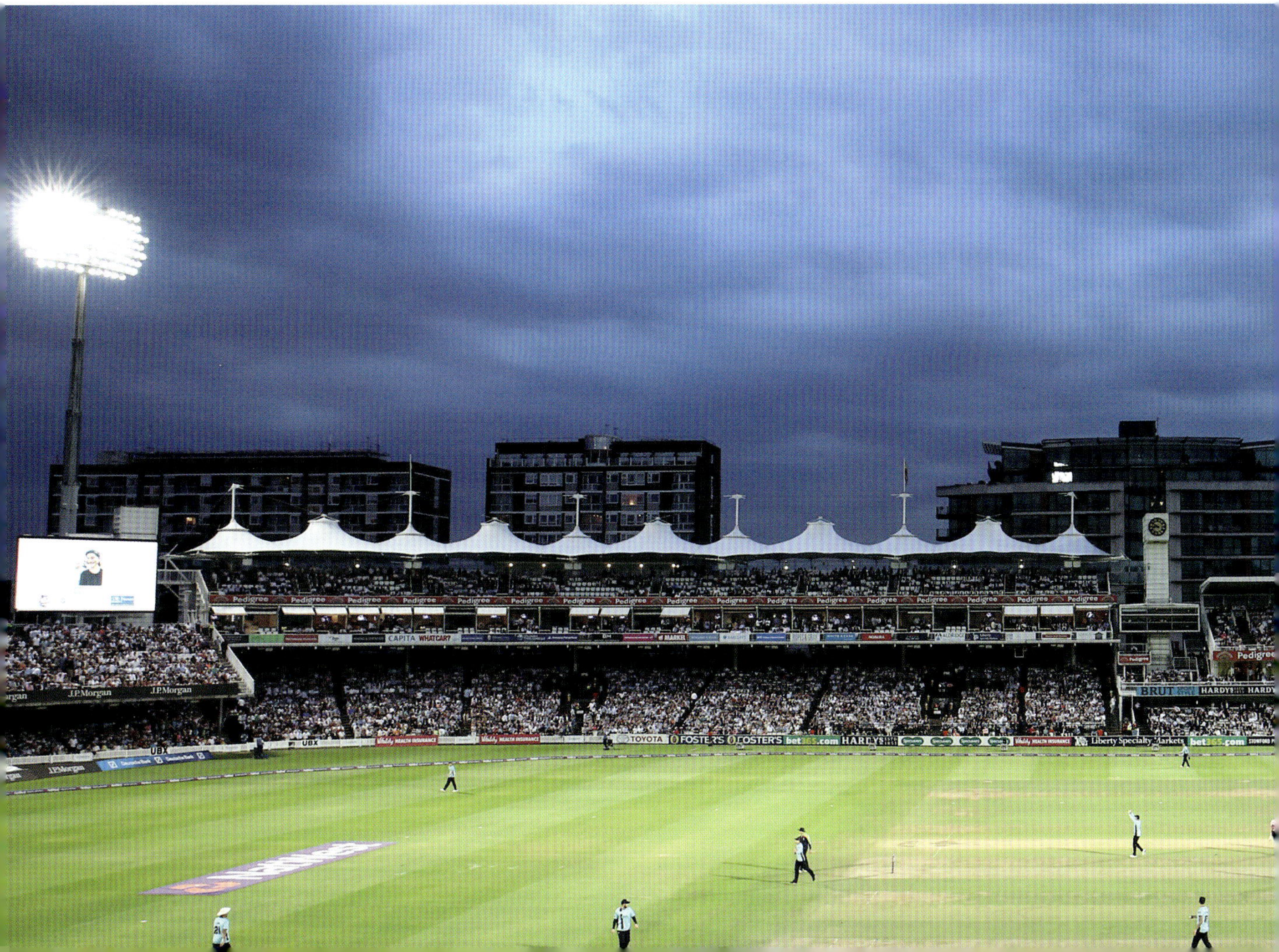

Richie Benaud to Neil Harvey on his first
visit to Lord's, 1953. Quoted in *Richie
Benaud, Anything But...an Autobiography*
(Hodder & Stoughton, 1998), p.74.

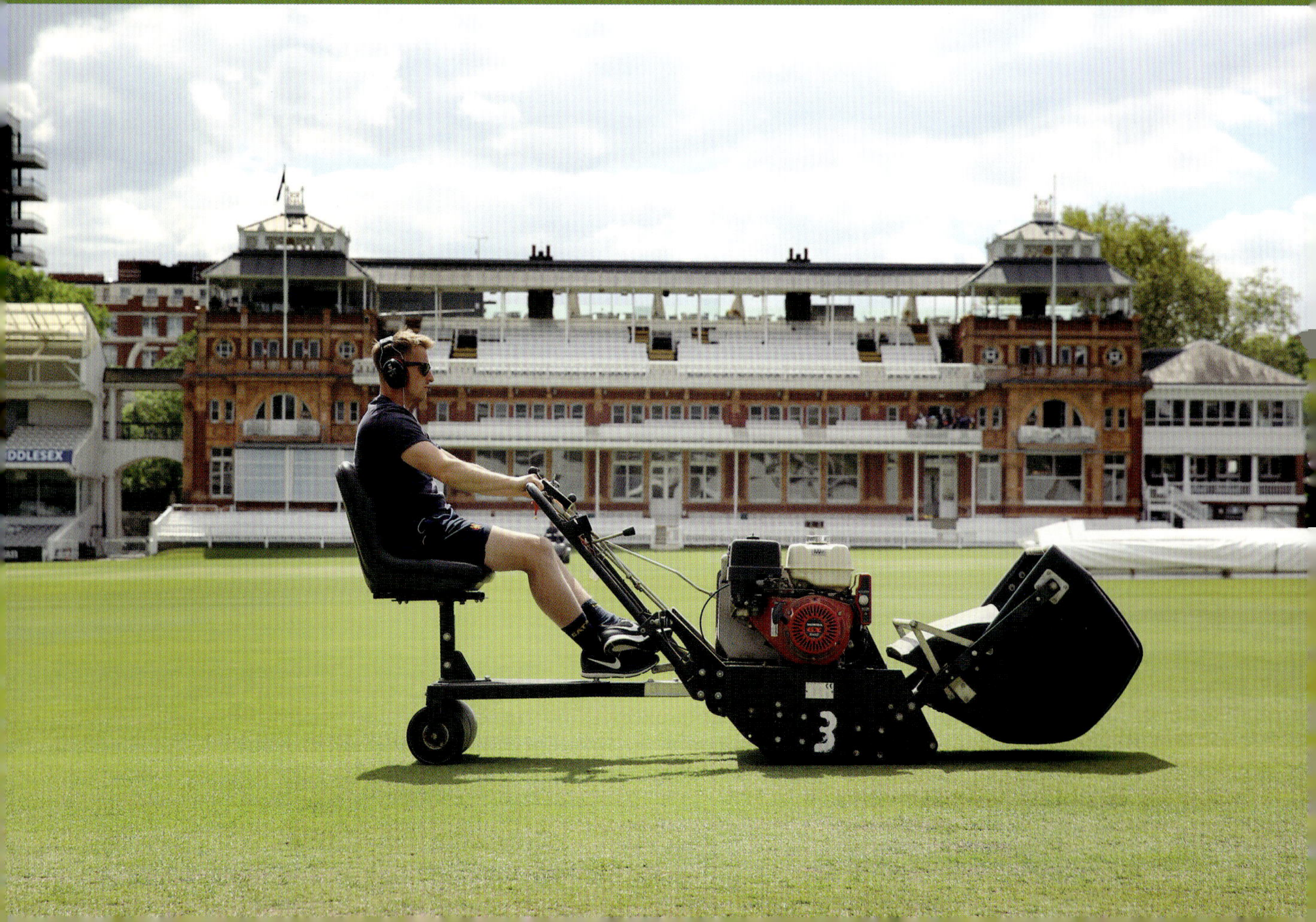

Below: Keeping the playing
surface in perfect condition
requires constant work
from the Lord's ground staff.
Lord's acquired its first
lawnmower in the 1860s;
prior to that the grass was
kept short by sheep.

Right: Temporary stands
and targets were set up
on the playing area during
the Archery tournament
of the London 2012
Olympic Games.

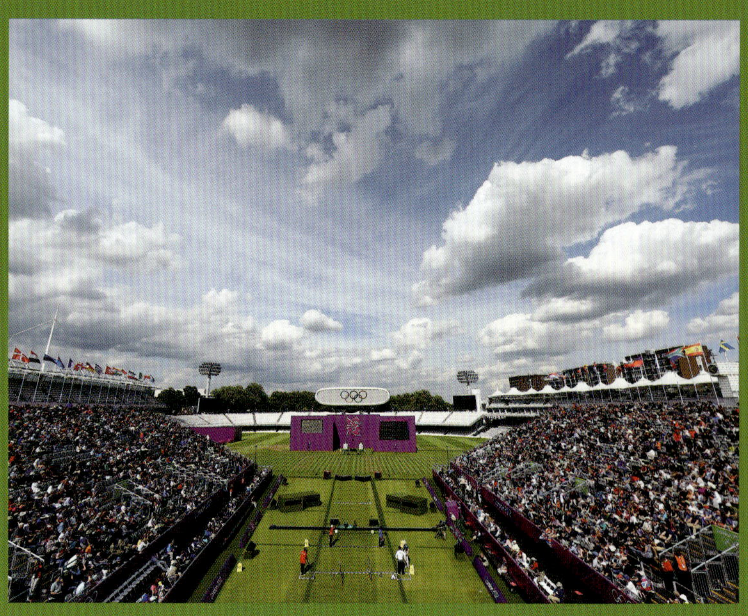

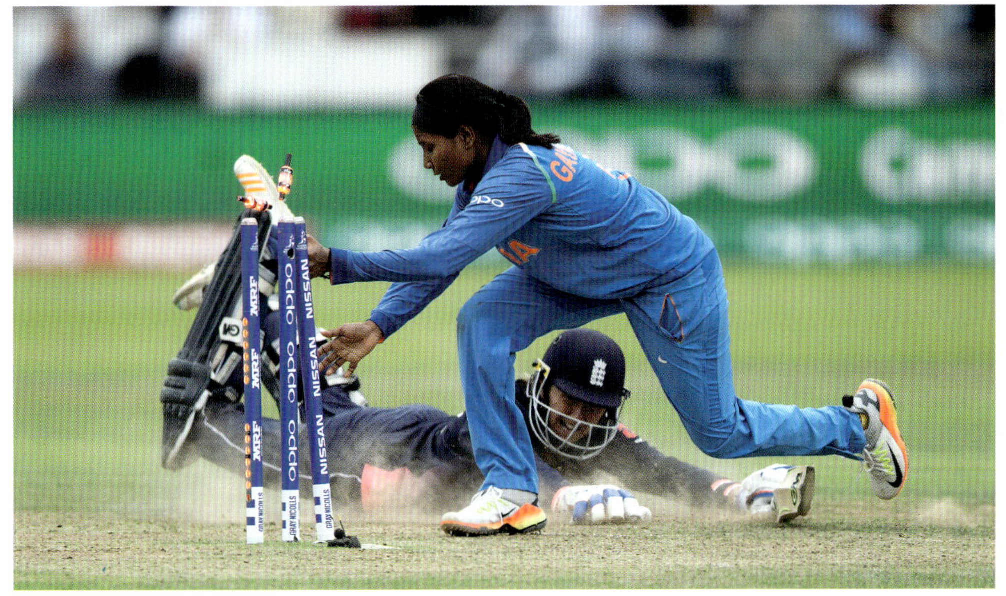

Left: India's Rayashwami Gayakwad tries to complete a run-out in the 2017 ICC Women's World Cup Final.

Below: Ground staff bring covers on to the wicket during the rain-affected 2018 England v India Test Match.

The Playing Area

Tradition says that each time Thomas Lord moved his ground he took the turf with him, and cricketers have always liked to imagine themselves treading in the footsteps of their illustrious predecessors. For much of the 19th century the Lord's pitch had a reputation for being poor and even dangerous; it also suffered from inadequate drainage.

In 2003 the entire main Ground – except for the playing square – was dug out and re-laid, and some 20,000 tons of London clay were removed. Deep drains and state-of-the-art sprinkler systems were introduced and topped with a specially selected turf. This presented MCC with a perfect opportunity to level the Ground's famous slope, which drops 2.5 m (6 ft 8 in) from north to south. However, history held sway – leaving cricketers still to face this unique challenge, whether as bowler, batsman or wicketkeeper.

The first Head Groundsman, David Jordan, was appointed in 1865. He has had only eight successors, the latest being Karl McDermott, newly installed in 2019. McDermott's predecessor Mick Hunt was in charge of the square from 1984 to 2018, having begun work at Lord's as an Assistant Groundsman in 1969.

Today more cricket than ever is played, but opportunities for spectators to walk on the hallowed turf are few and far between. Only on select days in very good weather is the crowd invited to 'perambulate'.

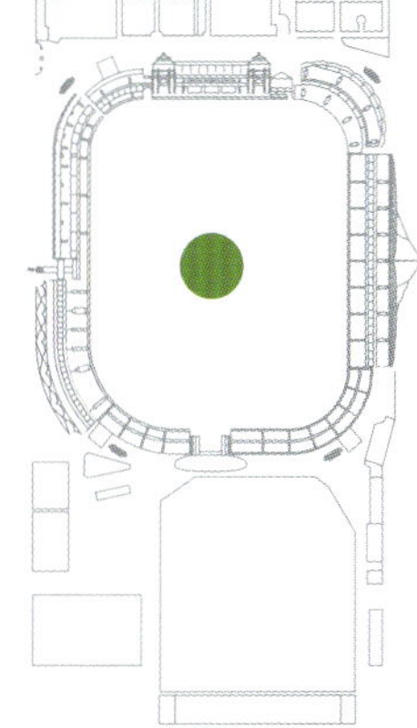

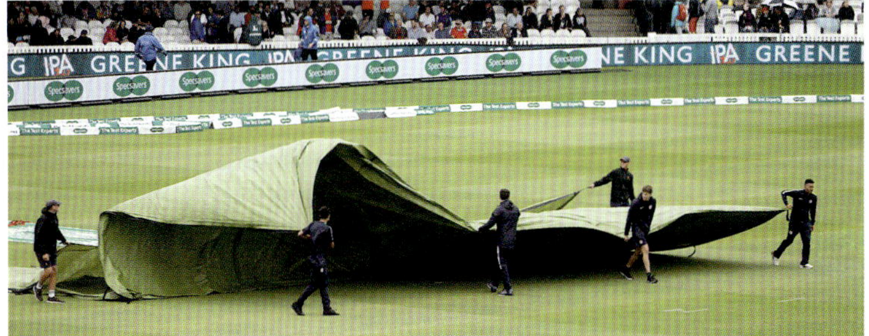

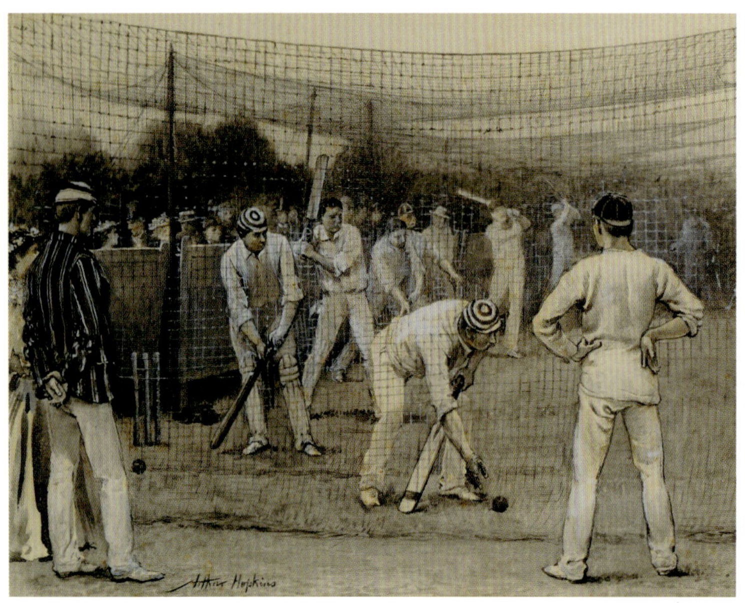

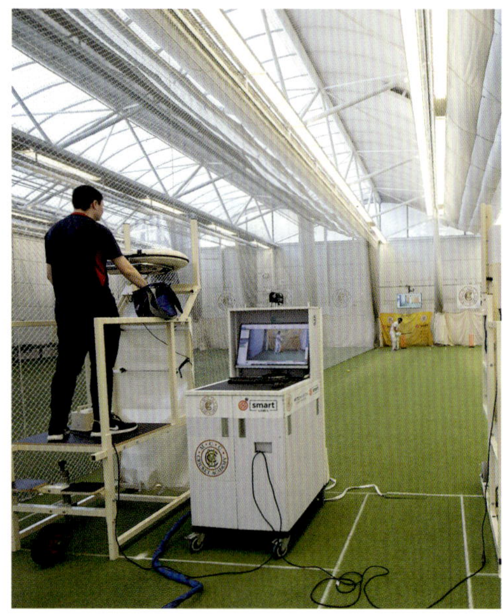

The Nursery Ground

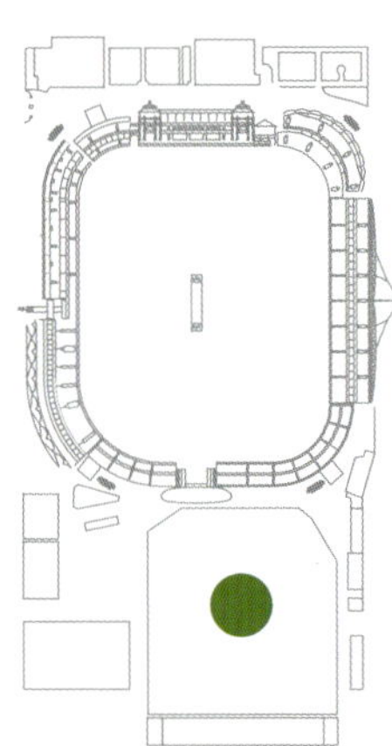

Behind the J.P. Morgan Media Centre is the 'Nursery' Ground. In the early years of Lord's, MCC Members had been allowed to practise by Henderson's Nursery, famed for the quality of its tulips and pineapples. In 1887, to celebrate the Club's centenary, the whole area (3.5 acres) was bought by MCC and converted into a practice area for cricket. It was subsequently surrounded by a chain of graceful arbours that were in great demand on social occasions.

MCC retains a long tradition of promoting youth cricket. Facing on to the Nursery Ground is the MCC Cricket Academy, where the famous Lord's Easter Coaching Classes (instituted by Sir Francis Lacey in 1902) take place. Designed by David Morley and opened in 1998, its concept was ground-breaking: a huge, uninterrupted space, lit by natural light from the ceiling and from doors that opened almost its full length. The new Academy won five awards and was runner-up for the prestigious Stirling Prize.

Above left: *Practising at the Nets, Lord's* by Arthur Hopkins, *c.*1900.

Above right: A bowling machine in use in the MCC Cricket Academy.

Right: Cross Arrows take on Trent Bridge on the Nursery Ground in September 2016.

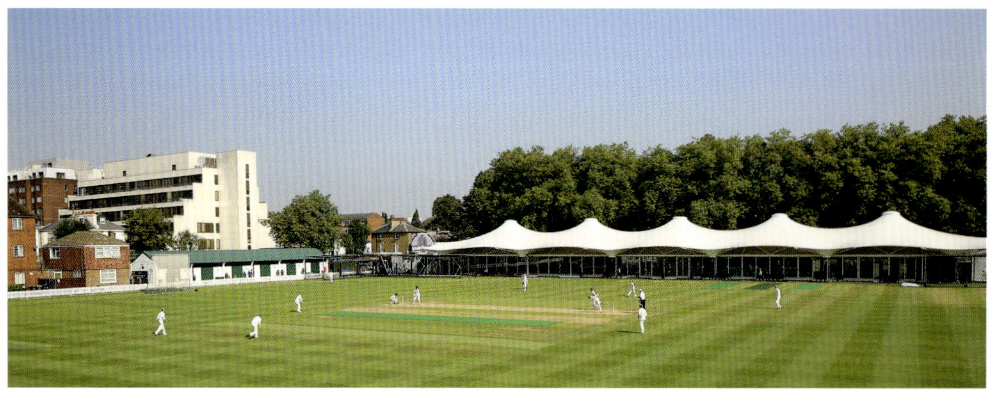

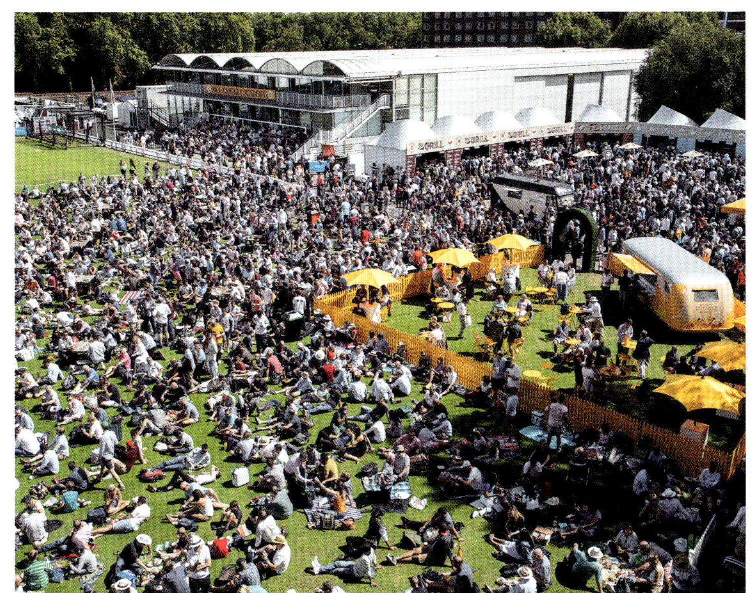

Left: A huge crowd enjoys the sunshine on the Nursery Ground and in the adjacent food village.

Below: Practice nets in use on the Nursery Ground, prior to the 2016 England v Sri Lanka Test Match.

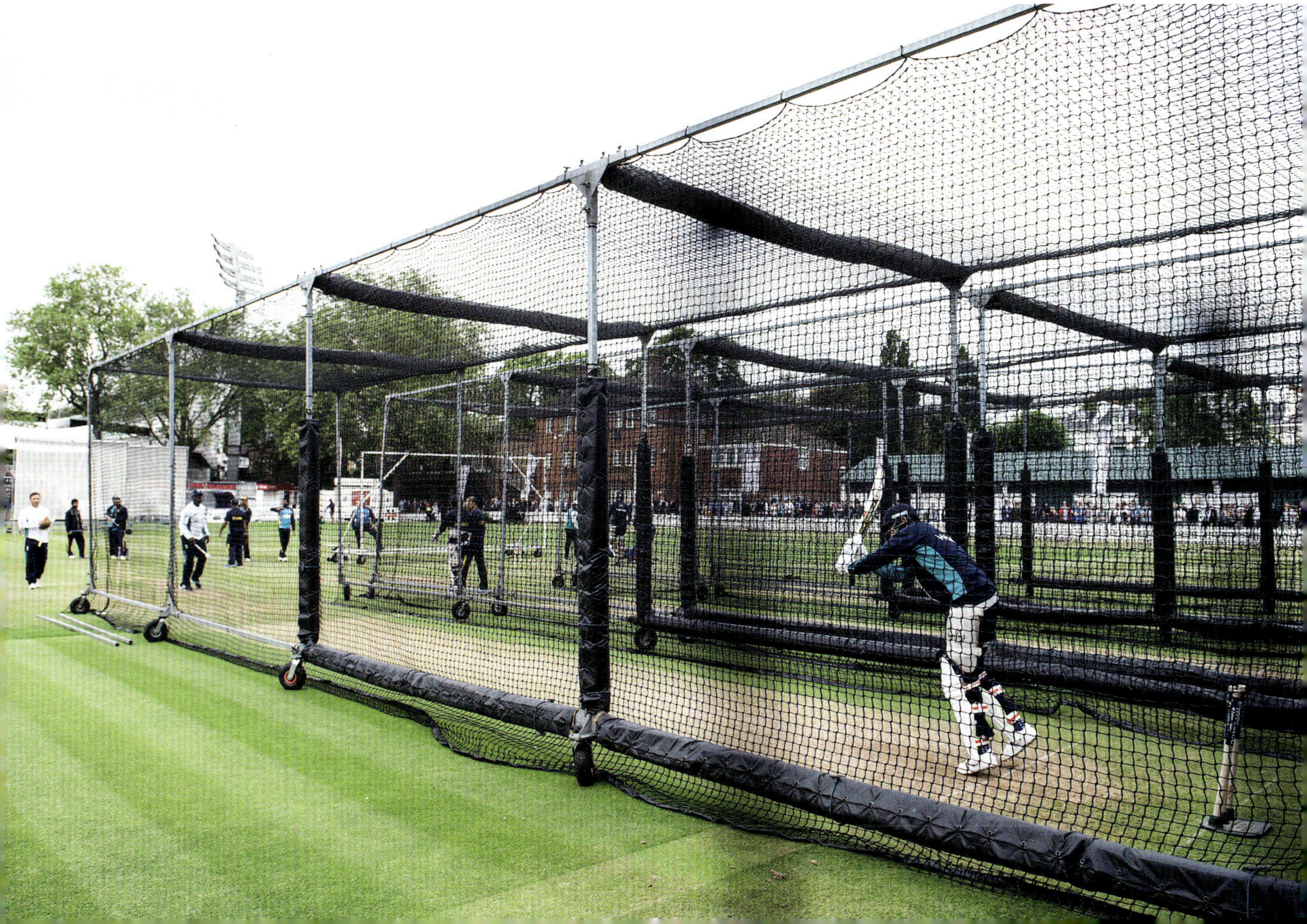

The Father Time Weather Vane

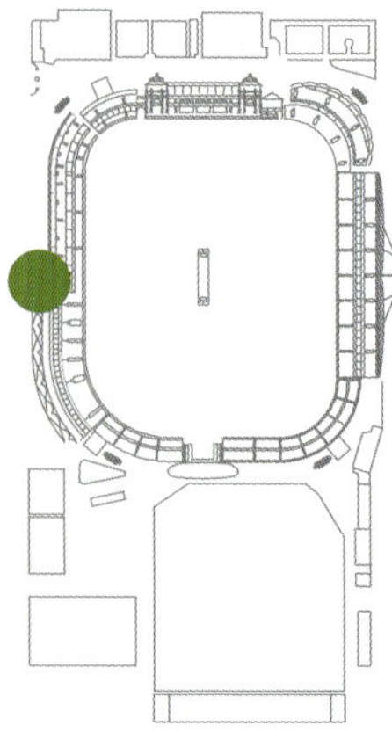

The Father Time weather vane, which has become such a well-known Lord's symbol, was a gift to MCC from Sir Herbert Baker, the architect of the second Grand Stand, completed in 1926. A total surprise to the MCC Committee, it was intended as compensation for the cost of the stand and its late completion.

The figure represented is the mythical Father Time character (similar to the Roman god Janus, after whom the month of January is named) who watches over the passage of time.

There has always been debate as to whether the figure is placing the bails at the start of a game or removing them at the end of a day's play.

The weather vane is around 6ft 6in (2m) tall in total. It is made of cast iron, which is painted black. Gilding features on the tip of the wind-arrow and the blade of Father Time's sickle.

Father Time was Lord's only casualty during the Second World War, when the cables of a drifting barrage balloon became entangled with the weather vane and wrenched it loose. He spent the remainder of the war housed safely in the Committee Room.

When Sir Herbert Baker's Grand Stand was demolished in 1996, Father Time was moved to his new home: on top of the lift shaft between the Mound and Tavern stands. From his new vantage point Father Time continues to watch over Lord's into the 21st century.

In the south-west corner of the Ground is the Tavern Stand, formerly the site of the much-loved Lord's Tavern. For almost a century the Tavern (originally called the Lord's Hotel) was the centre of Lord's catering and hospitality. From 1907 to 1950 catering at Lord's was run by the indefatigable George Portman, whose business prepared and served around 3,000 lunches and 6,000 teas each major match day. He also ran a bakery and confectioners. Portman's home-made ice cream, chocolates and other sweet treats proved so popular that queues of people stretched up St John's Wood Road on non-match days.

The Tavern was demolished in 1967 to make way for the new stand with its enlarged capacity and modern hospitality boxes. A new Tavern pub was built to the west of the Grace Gates, where it remains today.

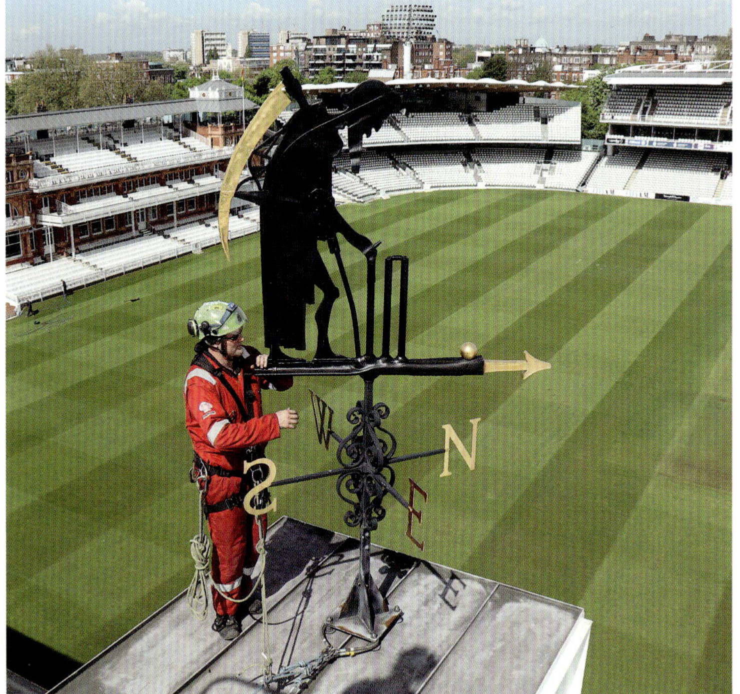

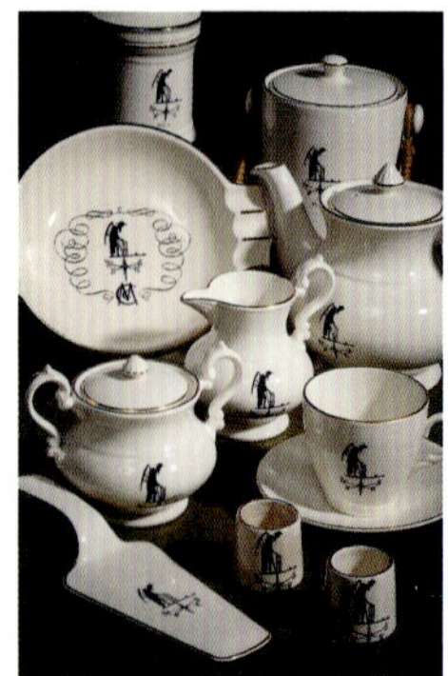

Left: Father Time is reinstalled in his traditional vantage point following conservation work in May 2018.

Right: Items from a 30-piece Father Time dinner and tea service. The set was produced by the Staffordshire ceramics company Lancaster & Sandland in the mid-20th century.

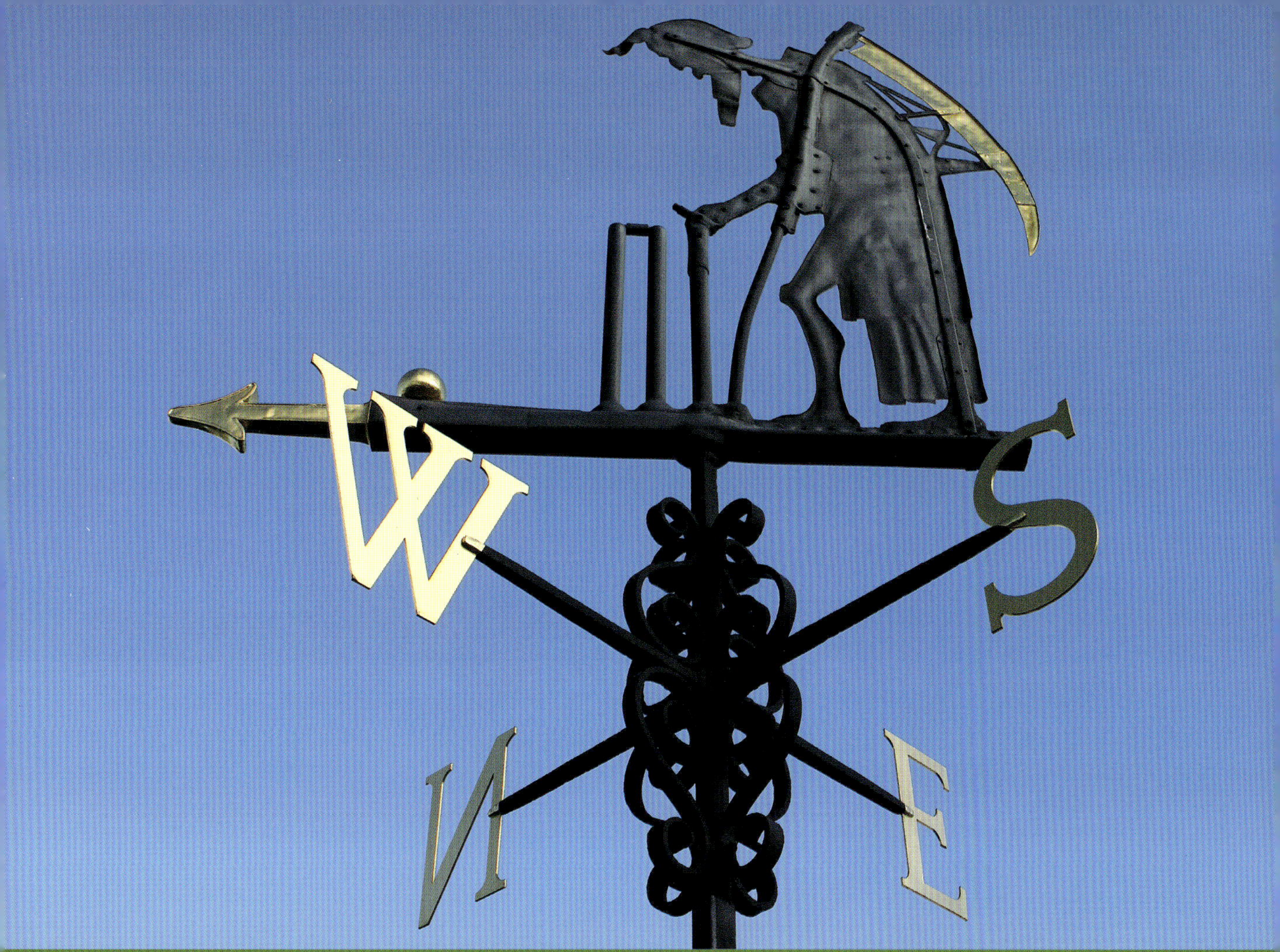

Above: A restored Father Time back in position between the Mound and Tavern Stands. Note the welding marks visible on his arm.

Right: The Lord's Tavern in a sketch by W.A. Bettesworth, *c.*1920. The Tavern was a much-loved feature of Lord's for 99 years before it was demolished to make way for the modern Tavern Stand.

'Lord's has something no other cricket ground quite possesses. There is an enveloping atmosphere of tradition and peace about the place.'

J.H. Fingleton, *The Ashes Crown the Year* (Collins, 1954)

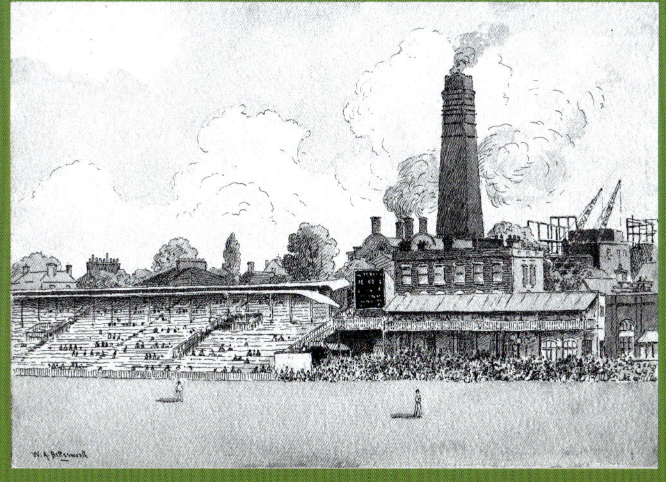

Right: *Portrait of Lord Harris* by Albert Chevallier Tayler, 1905. This is one of a series of action portraits Chevallier Tayler completed, based on the pioneering photography of George Beldam.

Far right: A statue of W.G. Grace by Louis Laumen, 1999, now situated opposite the Harris Garden.

Below: The Allen Stand with its prominent scoreboard, seen here from the Tavern Stand concourse during the Middlesex v Surrey T20 Vitality Blast match in July 2018.

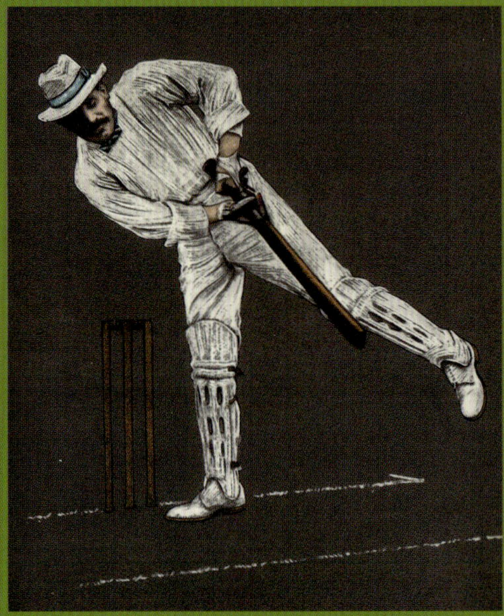

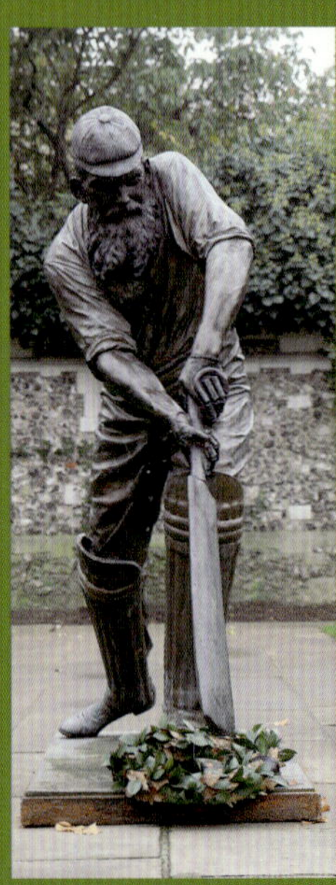

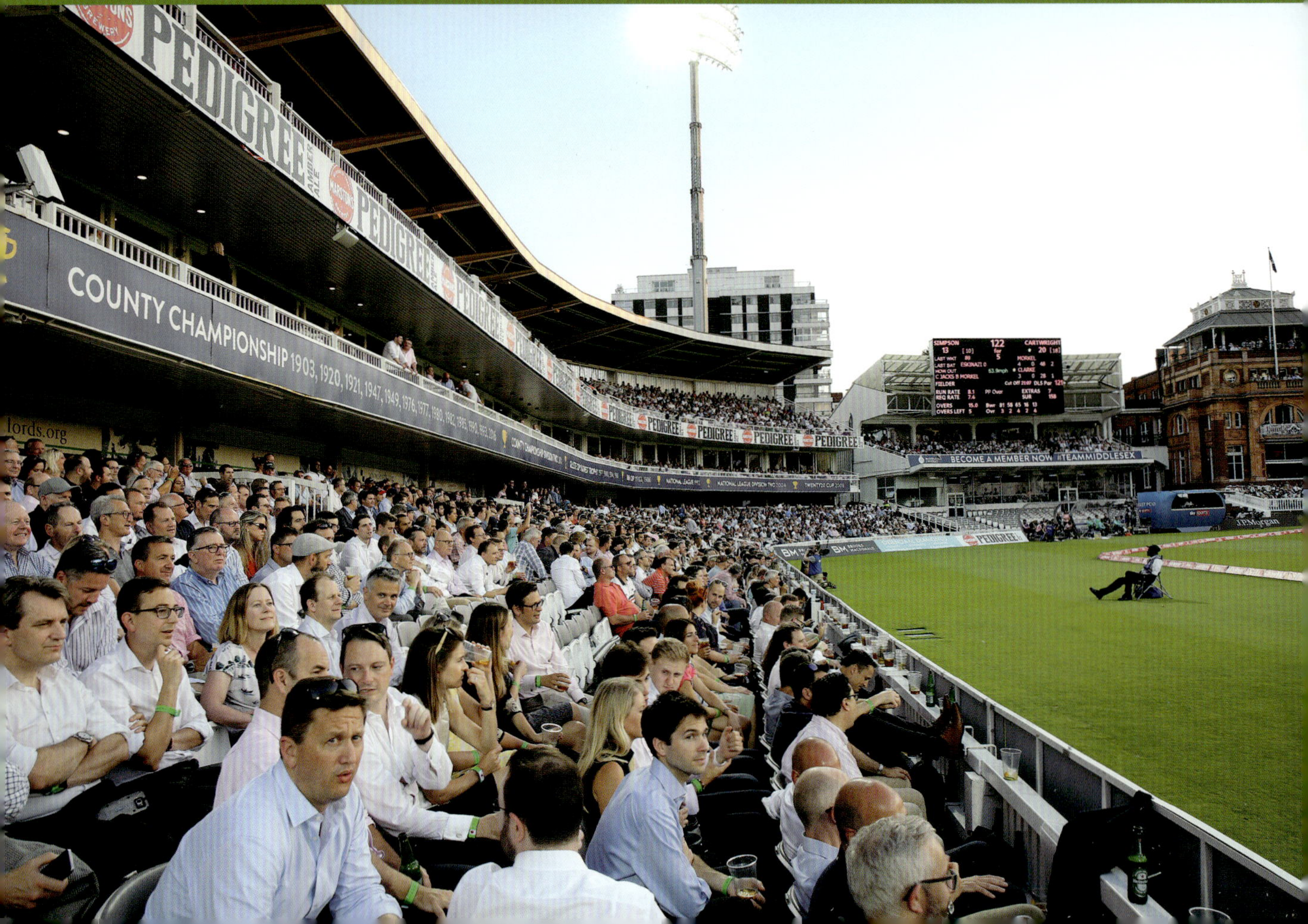

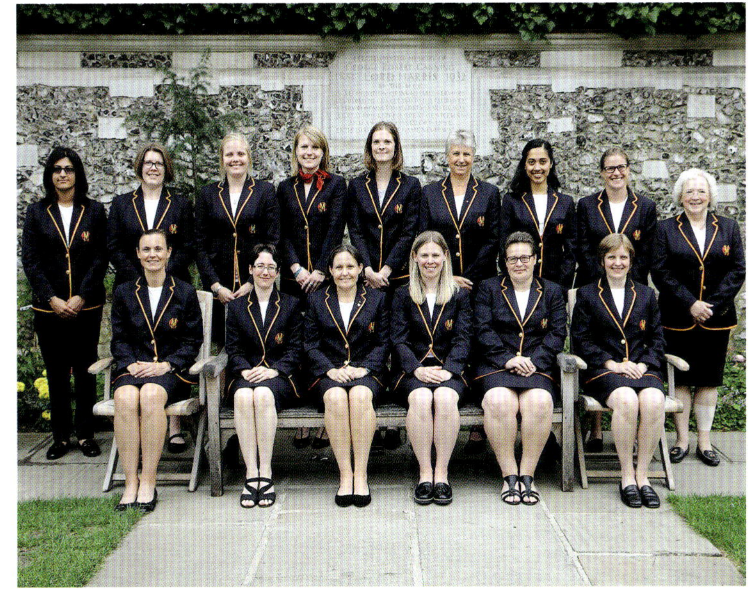

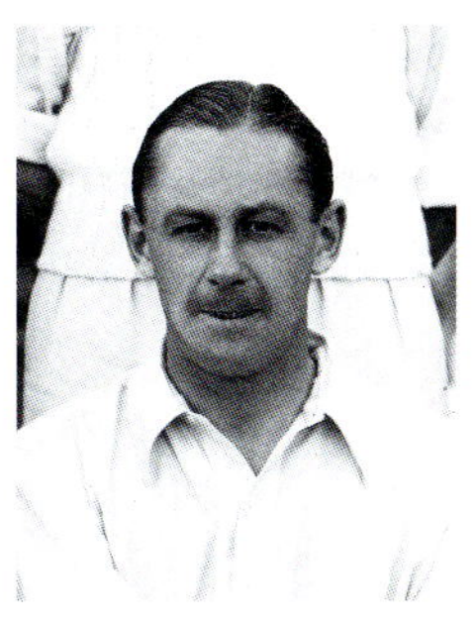

Allen Stand and Harris Garden

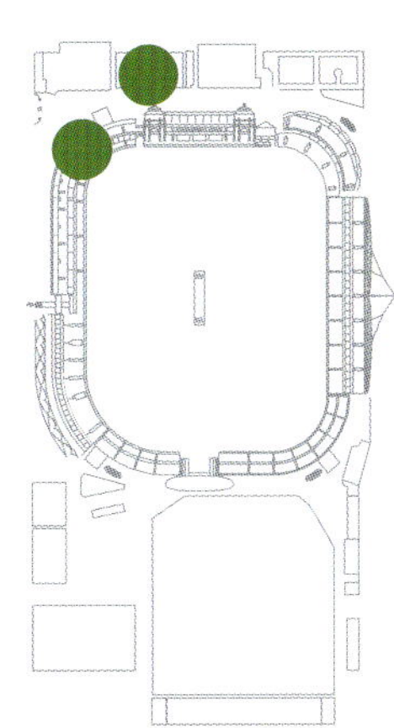

To the left of the Pavilion is the Allen Stand. Designed by Sir Herbert Baker and opened as 'Q' stand in 1934, it was refurbished and renamed in 1989 as a tribute to the Middlesex and England cricketer Sir George Allen (1902–89). His first-class career spanned 29 years and, after his playing days were over, 'Gubby' Allen remained closely involved with the game. He served as Chairman of Selectors from 1955–63, Chairman of the MCC Cricket Committee from 1956–63, MCC President in 1963–4 and Treasurer from 1964–76.

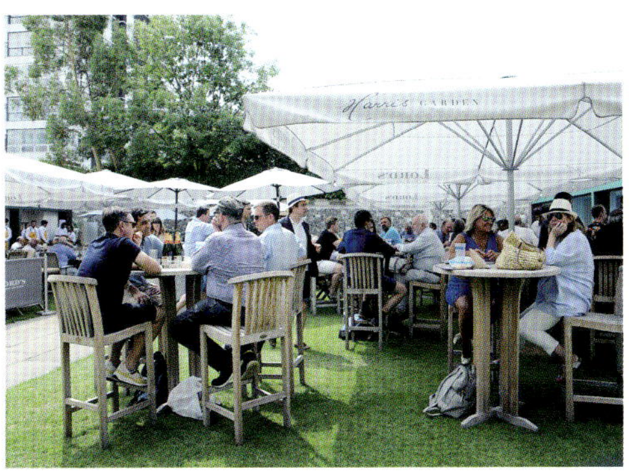

Behind the Allen Stand lies the Harris Garden. Originally the site of a lawn tennis court, the garden was laid out in 1934 in memory of the 4th Lord Harris (1851–1932). In a first-class career that spanned 41 years, Lord Harris captained Kent from 1871 to 1889 and led England in four Test Matches. He also led privately funded tours to North America in 1872 and Australia in 1878–9. Lord Harris became MCC President in 1895 and was Treasurer of the Club from 1916 to 1932. Away from the game he served in government as Secretary of State for India from 1885 to 1886 and Under-Secretary of State for War from 1886 to 1889.

It is to Lord Harris that we owe the phrase 'Lord's, the Home of Cricket', which formed part of the dedication in his 1921 memoir *A Few Short Runs*. The design for the garden was the work of Sir Herbert Baker, architect of the Grace Gates; the flint for the memorial wall came from Harris' own estate in Kent. The recent planting now includes flora from every Test-playing nation.

'When we have match'd our rackets to these balls
We will, in France, by God's grace, play a set
Shall strike his father's crown into the hazard.'

William Shakespeare, *Henry V* (Act I, Scene 2)

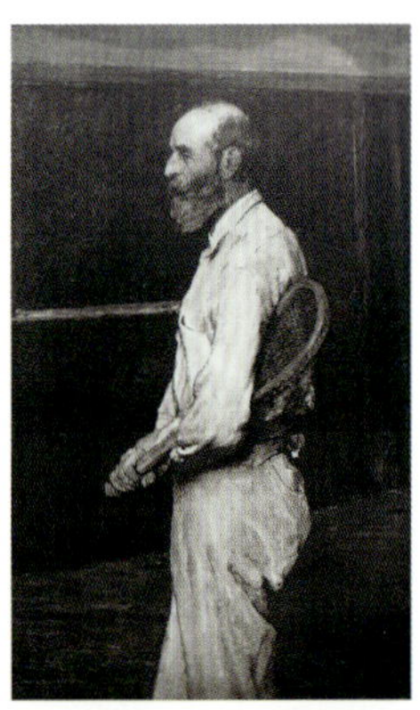

Left: Portrait of J.M. Heathcote, winner of the MCC Gold Racket 1867–81, 1883 and 1886.

Below: Action from the 2015 European Open Tennis Championship, held at Lord's.

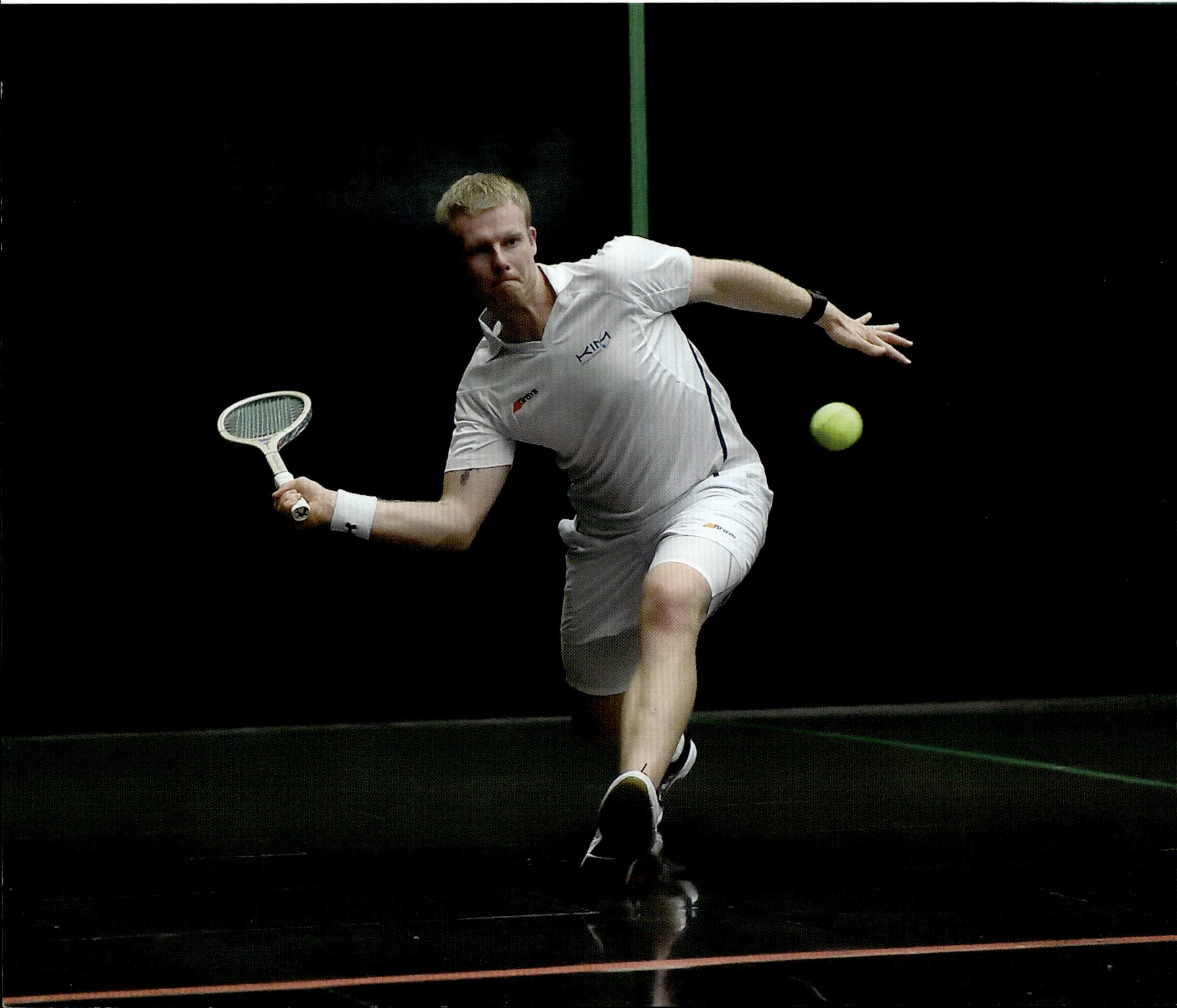

The Real Tennis Court

Over two centuries Lord's has hosted many games other than cricket, among them baseball, hockey, bowls and archery. Yet none has had such an enduring place in the life of the Ground as real tennis.

Over many centuries this was the favourite sport of French and English kings. Henry VII and Henry VIII were both keen players; the latter built several courts, including one at Hampton Court that is still in use today. Many people first hear of the game from Shakespeare, who mentions it in no fewer than five of his plays.

Lord's possesses one of the 24 real tennis courts in the country. Its first court was built on the site of the present Mound Stand in 1838. The present court was opened on 1 January 1900 and hosts many regular tournaments, including the Varsity match between Oxford and Cambridge and the European Open Singles Championship.

The game had its origins in medieval Europe. It is said that the court's seemingly eccentric shape, with its complicated grilles and galleries, derives from the contours of monastic cloisters where real tennis was played. To the uninitiated the game makes for strange viewing. The racket has remained largely unchanged for the last 200 years; its shape corresponds to the palm of the hand with which the ball was struck. The ball itself has a hard centre with a soft felt cover and less bounce than a lawn tennis ball. Real tennis combines physical activity with considerable subtlety. This means that it can be played to a high standard at an age beyond most racket games.

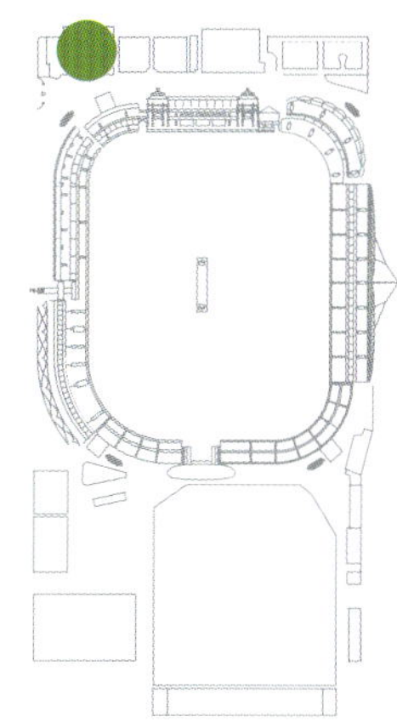

Below: A racket being strung in the MCC Tennis department. Real tennis rackets have a slightly different shape to those used for lawn tennis; the asymmetric, kidney-shaped head helps keep the sweet spot close to the floor for low-bouncing balls and gives a larger surface area with which to 'cut' the ball and impart backspin.

Right: The real tennis court at Lord's. When the new court was opened in 1900 the original flooring was transferred from the old court, with more worn areas being reinstalled close to the net. It is reputed to be one of the finest surfaces in the country.

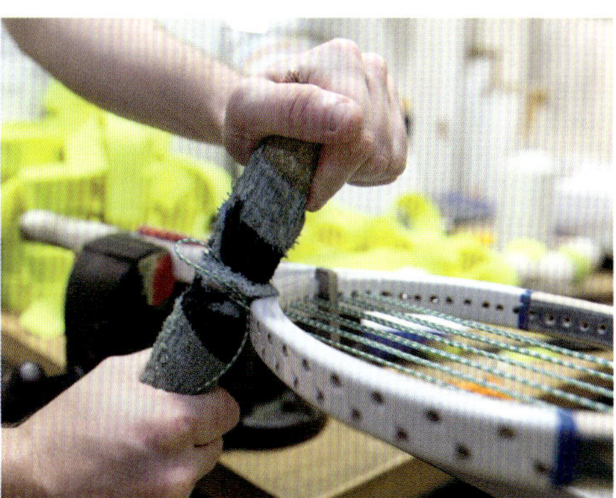

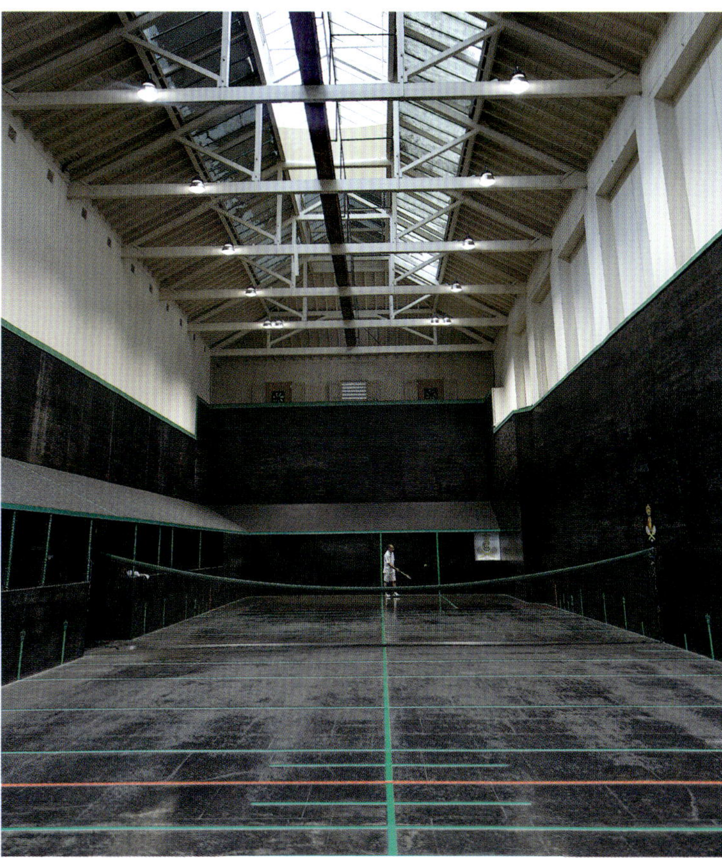

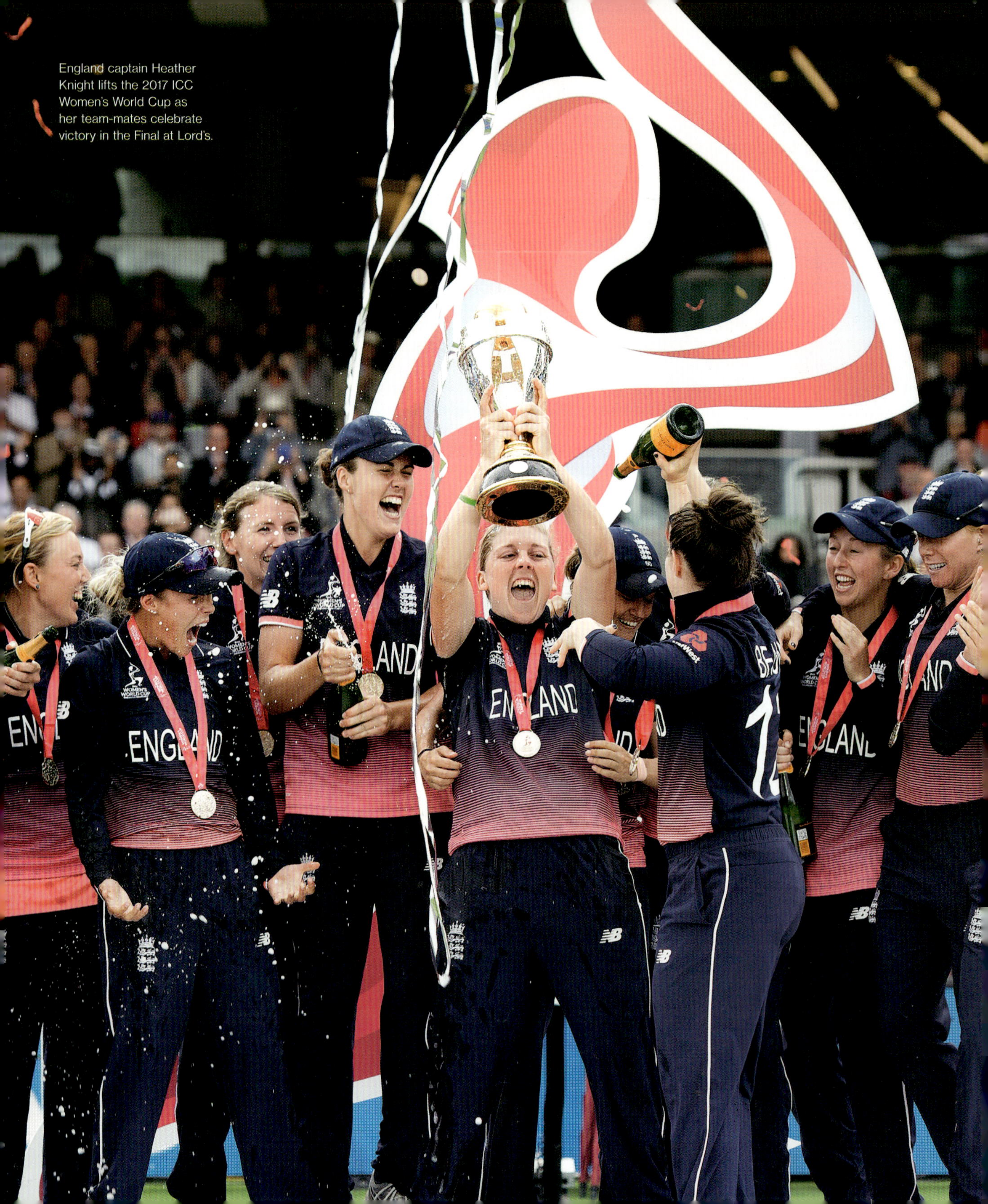

England captain Heather Knight lifts the 2017 ICC Women's World Cup as her team-mates celebrate victory in the Final at Lord's.